School Bells
and
Inkwells

Favorite School Stories and More!

DR. TEE CARR

Enjoy! Tee Carr

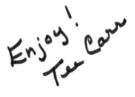

CARR
ENTERPRISES

We wish to acknowledge the following publishers and individuals for granting permission to reprint the following material:

Behold the Future. Reprinted by permission of Angie Martin. ©2000 Angie Martin.

When My Class Is the Greatest from *RECESS* by Elspeth Campbell Murphy. Reprinted by permission of Baker Book House, Grand Rapids, Michigan, 1992. ©1988 Elspeth Campbell Murphy.

For the "Why-Aren't-I-Doing-Anything-Important?" Blues from *CHALKDUST* by Elspeth Campbell Murphy. Reprinted by permission of Baker Book House, Grand Rapids, Michigan, 1989. ©1979 Elspeth Campbell Murphy.

All I Really Need to Know I Learned in Kindergarten excerpt from *All I REALLY NEED TO KNOW I LEARNED IN KINDERGARTEN* by Robert L. Fulghum. Reprinted by permission of Random House, Inc., New York. ©1986, 1988 Robert L. Fulghum.

(Continued on Page 307)

The names of students have been changed to protect their privacy.

Printed in the United States of America

First edition published in 2000

Library of Congress Catalog Card Number 00-105625
    Carr, Dr. Tee
        School Bells and Inkwells Favorite School Stories and More! A collection of favorite stories about teachers, students, and schools. For teachers, parents, students. First edition.

ISBN 1-892897-03-2 $14.95

Attention: Schools and Corporations
Books are available at volume discounts for educational, business, or sales promotional use. Please contact:

CARR Enterprises
3 Belvoir Circle
Chattanooga, TN 37412
Office: 423-698-5685
Fax: 423-698-3182
E-mail: drtcarr@aol.com

A Treasure Chest of School Stories

She might not like my English, but Dr. Tee Carr has gone and done it again! "School Bells and Inkwells" is another great book that will make teachers proud to be teachers and everyone else wish they were. If you're interested in education that informs the mind and inspires the soul, Tee is the place to be.

Dalton Roberts
The South's Downhome Philosopher

The stories in "School Bells and Inkwells" will inspire tears and laughter, love and hope, memories and self-reflection. They stand as true examples that teaching is a work of heart.

Vickie Honeycutt
North Carolina Regional Teacher of the Year

Dr. Tee Carr gets an A+ on her latest book, "School Bells and Inkwells." Truly, she is commended for her creativity and talent in combining into one book the favorite school stories written and experienced by people from all walks of life. The experiences shared through these stories are interesting and believable, as they are told by people (educators, parents, school volunteers) who play a major role in the lives of young people. They remind us of how important it is to be an educator and thus contribute to the growth and development of children and youth at all levels.

Dr. Clifford L. Hendrix, Jr.
Retired, Deputy Superintendent
Chattanooga Public Schools

For anyone who has ever taught . . . or has ever been a student . . . this delightful collection of anecdotes and observations is MUST reading!

Roger McCandless
Retired Educator . . . and Student

iii

"School Bells and Inkwells" is the perfect antidote to those negative and often frightening news stories about the condition of our schools. It serves to reassure parents that there truly are caring educators, and it encourages battle-weary teachers who genuinely love "their kids" and go the extra mile daily to hang in there. Teachers really do make a difference.

Al and Ann Musico
Parents
New York

Dedicated to
all the storytellers
who, through their generous contributions
to this book,
gave us a glimpse into
the wonderful world of teachers and children.

Stories carry us to special places and capture the true meaning of life. Schools, especially, generate hundreds and hundreds of stories each year. Many are hilarious; many are touching. Unfortunately school stories too often are not shared with others. After decades and decades of educational reform, we still have room for improvement. Maybe it's time to think about *restorying* our schools rather than constantly restructuring them.

Dr. Terrence E. Deal
Co-author of *Corporate Cultures*
and *Leading With Soul*

Books by Dr. Tee Carr

All Eyes Up Here!
A Portrait of Effective Teaching

How Come The Wise Men Are In The DEMPSTER DUMPSTER®?
A Celebration of Children

School Bells and Inkwells
Favorite School Stories and More!

Contents

ix

Acknowledgments

My sincere thanks are extended to all the people who sent me their favorite school stories. I can't tell you how exciting it was to find a new story in my mailbox or on my fax machine each day. You may read more about these talented individuals in the "Contributors" section of the book.

A special thanks goes to Marsha Brumlow who has worked with me on all three of my books. We spent many late night sessions on the computer fine-tuning the manuscript and preparing it for publication. Marsha's ideas, creativity, dedication, and loyalty to this project were priceless.

My deep appreciation goes to Sammy Gooden who gave me invaluable suggestions for improving the book and spent countless long hours proofreading and editing *School Bells and Inkwells*. Lending their help in this tremendous endeavor were Beth, Holly, and Tara Smithson, Paula and Pete Carnes, Mary Carnes, and my husband, Jack Carr.

In addition, I want to thank the people who gave me ideas for stories or leads to other individuals who had stories. My gratitude to Terry Smithson, Joe Bean, Mary Moore, Mildred Flynt, Beth and Pat Myers, Betty MacQueen, Roger McCandless, and Beth Smithson.

Thanks also to the many book, newspaper, and music publishing companies, journalists, songwriters, authors, and estate representatives of authors who worked with me so diligently to obtain permissions to reprint some of my favorite school stories which were found in other media.

My hat is off to the extraordinary people at the Chattanooga-Hamilton County Bicentennial Library whose research department was always ready and willing to assist me in the multitude of duties that are necessary in writing and publishing a book.

And last, but certainly not least, thanks to the members of my family who put up with a slightly "distracted" wife, daughter, mother, sister, aunt, and grandmother for over two years. They pretended not to notice or be bothered by my stacks and stacks of stories, papers, memos, to-do lists, permission forms, notebooks, letters, drawings, and other book-related confusion that cluttered up my home and life during this period. Their support and encouragement will always be treasured.

In my book, all of these special individuals deserve an A+!

Introduction

After I wrote *All Eyes Up Here!* and *How Come The Wise Men Are In The DEMPSTER DUMPSTER,* I was often invited as a guest speaker to schools, colleges, parent meetings, and educational conferences. During these visits, several teachers, parents, or students would invariably tell me a favorite story of theirs. Most were so impressive that I'd request that they jot the story down and mail it to me. Before long, I was receiving stories every day. I decided to preserve these in print, and this was the beginning of *School Bells and Inkwells.*

The stories in this book were written by people from all walks of life—from a first grade student in New York to a former FBI special agent in Atlanta, from a syndicated columnist in Chicago to a Congressman in Tennessee. There are stories from fathers, mothers, ministers, businessmen and women, teachers, principals, students, songwriters, newspaper journalists, and television personalities.

To these stories, I added a few of my own and obtained permission to include stories from books and other media that had great meaning to me in my career. You will enjoy Lewis Grizzard's touching narrative about his mother, Miss Christine, who was a first grade teacher. You'll laugh with Bill Cosby when he writes about his frustrating experiences trying to help his children with their homework. And you'll smile when you read Oprah's candid words about how she admired her fourth grade teacher and wanted to be just like her when she grew up.

Not all the stories are happy ones. Some are about children that have, to our dismay, "slipped through the cracks"—children whom we have sadly failed. You have only to read "Cipher in the Snow" and "Jake, the Lost One" to see what I mean. There are, however, lessons to be learned from these stories— lessons that may prevent these tragedies from happening again.

Some authors wrote about a particular student or teacher who had a tremendous impact on their lives and attached notes to their stories. One author wrote, "I feel good that I finally had the chance to write about this exceptional person." Another said: "This story needs to be told. Thanks for giving me the opportunity to get it out to the people who may be helped by it." A few authors thought the writing of their story was a cathartic experience. One said, "A load has been lifted from me by the telling of my story." Another said that his story had been "bouncing around in his mind" for years and that "it did me good to finally put it down on paper."

The stories in *School Bells and Inkwells* demonstrate, for the most part, that we have exceptional teachers and other school personnel working with our young people. These individuals go far beyond their job descriptions on a daily basis. Take a moment to read "Assignment: School Patrol" to see what I mean. From these stories we experience positive feelings about the future of our children and our nation.

There are over a hundred stories in *School Bells and Inkwells*. Place this book on your nightstand beside your bed where you can easily reach it. Take time to savor the stories and think about their meaning and relevance.

School bells are ringing! They signal that class is about to begin. Please open your book to page one and enjoy this treasure chest of stories about students, teachers, and classrooms.

Foreward

School stories usually center on students, teachers, parents, classroom instruction, discipline, communication, humor, and love, for it takes all of these working together to form the foundation of a good school.

Good school stories inspire, encourage, guide, nurture, motivate, and entertain. They instruct and enlighten individuals outside the organization. They reinforce the core values and basic beliefs shared by the members within the organization.

Stories give us the opportunity to view the activities taking place inside the school and discover what the individuals there hold near and dear to them. They give meaning and value to everyday life.

Stories often run the gamut of emotions. Some stories touch our funnybones; others touch our hearts. Still others reach into our very souls and cause us to become better people. As Lewis Carroll wisely said, "Stories are love gifts." These stories are our gifts for you.

Part I

CLASSROOMS

*A school should not be a preparation
for life. A school should be life.*
Elbert Hubbard
American Author and Publisher

Welcome to the World of Children

Welcome to the world of children;
Listen to the sounds of play!
Squeals of laughter,
Noisy chatter,
Fill each hour of every day.

You'll find in the world of children
Smells that bring back memories:
Maple pralines,
Chewy jelly beans.
Help yourself to all of these.

Welcome to the world of children.
See the way the stage is set:
Circus clowns and
Merry-go-rounds,
Sights and sounds you won't forget.

Join us in the world of children;
Park that frown beside the door.
Toss your fears,
Your hurts and tears.
You won't need them anymore.

Welcome to the world of children!
You'll enjoy a brand new start.
Just wear a grin,
You'll fit right in,
For you are still a kid at heart.

Tee Carr

Behold the Future

In they wander—some dressed, shoes shining; others ragged and torn. They sit down at desks and look to see if they know anyone sitting next to them. Then they look up at me. I smile and hope my smile puts them at ease and projects all the love I already feel for each of them. They don't know it yet, but when they walk out my door for the final time in June, they will know that they are *somebody.*

Each year new children will sit in my classroom: new chances, new hopes, new dreams for the future. Amazingly, I have been allowed to play a part in each of these lives. People in society wonder what the future holds. I tell them to come into my classroom and behold the future—children who believe that they can make a difference. Their knowledge can and will carry each of us into tomorrow.

Many years from now, I know I will be sitting back watching the news, and there will be "my kids" making this world a better place to be. There is hope when you look into the eyes of a child. I have seen it. I believe it, and I teach it.

Angie Martin

When My Class Is the Greatest

Father, sometimes I call them to line up, and
trailing clouds of glory do they come
from the playground,
not quarreling,
but laughing and eager
to get back to work.
And sometimes I can't believe
how good they are.
And I think,
"This is it.
This is what it's all about.
And I can walk with kings,
because I am a *teacher*
and these are my sweet, beautiful students!"
But then I think,
"They've got to be up to something, right?"

Elspeth Campbell Murphy

For the "Why-Aren't-I-Doing-Anything-Important?" Blues

Oh, Father,
How small this world of the classroom is,
bounded by alphabet charts and chalkboards,
bookcases and maps.

And how far this world seems
from the adult circles of money and prestige.
While other adults work together in those circles,
I am alone
among a throng of scurrying, chattering little people.

Little people and little things.
My days are so filled with little things.

Today I handed out a ream of kleenex,
marched a miscreant to the principal's office,
and put up a new bulletin board.

What am I doing here?
Why aren't I doing anything exciting and important
in the grownup world?

But, Father, there were *other* "little things" today.

Today Kevin came up to me,
bubbling with excitement,
and said,
"I can read this whole book all by myself!"

Today Michelle wrote a story that said:
"My dog is brown and white. He is a very nice
person."

Today Kathleen,
who has hardly said two words all year,
raised her hand to answer a question.

Perhaps years from now
I'll learn the results of these "little things"
that happened today.
Perhaps I won't.
But, Father, teach me to take delight in little things,
and never, never let me doubt their importance.

Elspeth Campbell Murphy

All I Really Need to Know I Learned in Kindergarten

All I really need to know about how to live and what to do and how to be I learned in kindergarten. Wisdom was not at the top of the graduate-school mountain, but there in the sandpile at Sunday School. These are the things I learned:

Share everything.
Play fair.
Don't hit people.
Put things back where you found them.
Clean up your own mess.
Don't take things that aren't yours.
Say you're sorry when you hurt somebody.
Wash your hands before you eat.
Flush.
Warm cookies and cold milk are good for you.
Live a balanced life—learn some and think some and draw and paint and sing and dance and play and work every day some.
Take a nap every afternoon.
When you go out into the world, watch for traffic, hold hands and stick together.

Be aware of wonder. Remember the little seed in the Styrofoam cup. The roots go down and the plant goes up and nobody really knows how or why, but we are all like that.

Goldfish and hamsters and white mice and even the little seed in the Styrofoam cup—they all die. So do we.

And then remember the Dick-and-Jane books and the first word you learned—the biggest word of all—LOOK.

Everything you need to know is in there somewhere. The Golden Rule and love and basic sanitation. Ecology and politics and equality and sane living.

Take any one of those items and extrapolate it into sophisticated adult terms and apply it to your family life or your work or your government or your world and it holds true and clear and firm. Think what a better world it would be if we all—the whole world—had cookies and milk about three o'clock every afternoon and then lay down with our blankies for a nap. Or if all governments had as a basic policy to always put things back where they found them and to clean up their own mess.

And it is still true, no matter how old you are—when you go out into the world, it is best to hold hands and stick together.

Robert Fulghum

Pat Conroy had almost completed his second year in education when he applied for the teaching position on Yamacraw Island. Yamacraw is a small island off the South Carolina mainland not far from Savannah, Georgia. It was sparsely populated by a few poor families whose ancestors had lived there for generations. The two-room schoolhouse was totally isolated from the outside world, and Conroy found that the eighteen children in his class were practically illiterate. He set out to introduce his students to the excitement of learning and the joy of success.

Excerpt from
The Water Is Wide

"O.K., gang, loosen up. Shake those hands and feet. We are going to dust the cobwebs off those sweet little brains of ours. Prophet, you are going to have the opportunity to prove that you are a genius before all the world today. Carolina, you are going to shine like the sun. Everybody is going to look good."

One of the questionable themes developed in two years of teaching was the necessity to put students at complete ease. It worked well in Beaufort, but the Yamacraw kids looked at me as though I were a mentally deficient clown.

"What country do we live in, gang? Everybody tell me at once," I exhorted.

No one said a word. Several of the kids looked at each other and shrugged their shoulders.

"Gang," I continued, "what is the name of this grand old, red, white, and blue country of ours? The place where we live. The land of the free and the home of the brave."

Still there was silence.

I was struggling for the right words to simplify the question even further. "Does anyone know what country we live in?" I asked again.

No one answered. Each child sat before me with a pained and embarrassed look.

"Have you ever heard of the United States of America?" I asked.

"Oh, yeh," Mary, one of the eighth-grade girls said. "I heared it. I heared it in I Pledge a legent to the flag of United States of America."

"The Pledge of Allegiance. Good, Mary. Then you know what country you live in."

"No, just know pledge a legent."

"All right, gang. Now the first golden nugget of information we are going to learn this year is that all of us live in the United States of America. Now the next thing I want someone to tell me is this: who is President of the United States in this year of 1969?" Again there was silence.

"Does anyone know?" I asked.

Everyone shook his head. Frank raised his hand. "John F. Kennedy," he said.

"Yeh," the whole class answered, looking to me for approval.

"Yeh," I responded. "That's great, Frank. Why did you say Kennedy?"

"He good to colored man," answered Frank.

"Yeh," the class answered.

"Yeh," I agreed.

"Can anyone tell me who the first President of the United States was?"

Silence again.

"Ever hear of George Washington?" I asked.

Only a couple of students nodded their heads affirmatively. The rest had not.

"Who can tell me who Willie Mays is?"

No one could.

"All right, gang, relax. We are going to get off these goofy people for a while. I am sick and tired of talking about people. Let's talk about water. Who can name me an ocean?"

Fred looked at Top Cat and Top Cat looked at Fred, who was staring intently at me. None of them had ever heard of any ocean.

"I'm going to give you a hint," I said, "one of the oceans washes up against the shore of Yamacraw Island."

Cindy Lou lit up and shouted, "Oh, he mean the beach."

"That's right, Cindy. Now what is the name of the beach?"

"The beach, man," she answered indignantly.

"No, I mean the name given to that whole ocean."

"I tole you it was the beach," she said angrily.

"O.K. It's the beach," I agreed. "But it also is

called the Atlantic Ocean. Have any of you ever heard it called that?"

All heads shook sadly and mournfully.

"Well, don't worry about it," I continued. "That kind of stuff is easy to learn. Just by talking about it, without even thinking real hard, you have learned what ocean is by Yamacraw. Mary, if I were a stranger on this island and I met you on the beach and asked you what body of water this was I was walking next to, what would you tell me?"

"Body?" she asked in a tone intimating that she had incriminating evidence against my sanity.

"Yeh, body of water."

"I don't know about no bodies," she insisted.

"Forget about body. What ocean would you tell me I was walking by?"

"Lantic Ocean."

"Atlantic."

"Atlantic," she repeated.

"What ocean, everybody?"

"Atlantic Ocean," they shouted in unison.

"Are you sure it's the Atlantic Ocean?"

"Yeh," they answered.

"Well, it's not."

They looked at me again like they had been placed under the jurisdiction of a functioning cretin.

"The real name of the ocean is the Conroy Ocean."

"No," they said.

"Yeh," I said.

"No," they said.

"Yeh, it's the truth. My great-great grandfather was Ferdinand Conroy, a Spanish soldier of fortune, who swam from Europe to North America, a distance of fifteen million miles. Because of this singular and extraordinary feat, they named this huge expanse of water after him."

"What you say?" one of the twins asked me.

"He didn't say nothen," Cindy Lou said.

"Anyway," I continued undaunted, "from that day forward, it has been called Conroy Ocean."

"No," George said.

"How do you know?" I challenged.

"Just ain't. You said it is Atlantic."

"I'm a liar."

"You's a teacher."

"Teachers lie all the time."

"Oh, Gawd," Lincoln said. I had been noticing whenever Lincoln was surprised or ecstatic, he would use the phrase *Oh Gawd*.

So the day continued and with each question I got closer and closer to the children. With each question I asked I got madder and madder at the people responsible for the condition of these kids. At the end of the day I had compiled an impressive ledger of achievement. Seven of my students could not recite the alphabet. Three children could not spell their names. Eighteen children thought Savannah, Georgia, was the largest city in the world. Savannah was the only city any of the kids could name. Eighteen children had never seen a hill—eighteen children had never heard the words *integration* and *segregation*. Four children could not add two plus two. Eighteen children did not know we were fighting a war in Southeast Asia. Of course, eighteen children never had heard of Asia. One child was positive that John Kennedy was the first President of the United States. Seventeen children agreed with that child. Eighteen children concurred with the pre-Copernican Theory that the earth was the center of the universe. Two children did not know how old they were. Five children did not know their birth dates. Four children could not count to ten. The four oldest thought the Civil War was fought between the Germans and the Japs.

Each question I asked opened up a new lesion of ignorance or misinformation. A stunned embarrassment gripped the class, as if I had broken some unwritten law by prying into areas where I had no business, or exposing linen of a very personal nature. No one would look me in the eye. Nor would anyone talk to me. I had stumbled into another century. The job I had taken to assuage the demon of do-gooderism was a bit more titanic than anticipated. All around the room sat human beings of various sizes and hues who were not aware that a world surrounded them, a world they would be forced to enter, and enter soon.

. . . And it was in this way that the pep-rally method of education began on Yamacraw Island. For the next several weeks a certain part of the morning was set aside for a daily chant or incantation to the gods of basic knowledge.

. . . And so it went. Whenever we learned something new, it became part of the pep rally. I would often go to the map and point to a country, or a continent, or a river or ocean, and ask them to identify it. The map itself became a center of class activity— the map, a symbol of the world, where Yamacraw was not even a pinprick, not even represented by a molecular dot when compared to the incomprehensible vastness of the world.

"Here is Asia and here is Yamacraw," I would chant, moving my finger along the map. "Here is California and here is Yamacraw. Here is China and here is Yamacraw. Gang, do you realize the neat things that are happening out there? The millions and millions of people swarming all over the earth? We are going to learn great stuff this year. We are going to stuff our brains with facts and ideas, and we are going to become sharp as razors."

Pat Conroy

Everyone Needs a Cubby

I don't remember when I first heard the word "cubby," but I do remember how I felt when I heard it.

Some words give me a special feeling. Cubby is one of those words.

There are many words, I'm sorry to say, that are cold words. These are words that do bad things to your mind, body, and especially your spirit.

Hate is a cold word.
Fear is a cold word.
Hurt, fight, kill, scream, and mean are cold.

Love is a warm word.
Safe is a warm word.
Fuzzy, soft, baby, kittens, and mittens are warm.

Cubby is a warm word.

A cubby is a place that holds all the things that mean something to you. It is a safe, warm place that belongs only to you.

In kindergarten, you have a cubby. It is where you keep your coat, mittens, and rainboots. It is where you place your lunch box, snack-time cookies, and favorite drawings. There is even room for your teddy bear and blanket.

As you grow bigger, so does your cubby.

It becomes your room, then your classroom, then your school. It can grow to be your town and country. And then your work. It should always be your home and family.

It is a warm, safe place that holds and protects all the precious things that give meaning to life.

Everyone needs a cubby.

Tee Carr

Homework Machine

The Homework Machine, oh the Homework Machine,
Most perfect contraption that's ever been seen.
Just put in your homework, then drop in a dime,
Snap on the switch, and in ten seconds' time,
Your homework comes out, quick and clean as can be.
Here it is—"nine plus four?" and the answer is "three."
Three?
Oh me . . .
I guess it's not as perfect
As I thought it would be.

Shel Silverstein

Remember Me

It was my third year teaching fourth grade, and I was complaining again because I did not have a wall map of Tennessee. One day during our social studies lesson, my principal walked into the room carrying a long brown box. Yes! It was a spring roller wall map of Tennessee with overlays and everything. The whole class was excited. The custodian installed it that afternoon.

Now I should explain that this was the late sixties, and shirtdresses were the fashion of the day. In case you don't remember, these were long-sleeve dresses that looked like men's button-down collar shirts, only longer. The day after our beautiful map was installed, I chose to wear my new dress.

When I pulled the map down the first time, I noticed that the spring mechanism was extremely tight. I didn't have time to adjust it because it was time to talk about the three grand divisions of Tennessee, and it was wonderful to have such a colorful representation. I did not notice as I stood in front of the map teaching that the pulldown hook was pointed up. As I turned to point out Memphis, my elbow hit the map and the next thing I knew, I was standing in front of my fourth grade class with both arms in the air. The only parts of my new blue shirtdress that I was still wearing were the buttoned cuffs on the sleeves. The rest of my dress was rolled up in the map above my head.

I will never forget the shocked look on the faces of my students, but there was not a sound or movement in the room. Very calmly, I asked a tall young man on the front row to come up and pull the map down. He turned his face and tried to reach up without looking at his teacher who was standing there in her slip. (Thank goodness for slips!) He unrolled the map, releasing my dress. I quickly dressed, and we went on with our lesson.

That afternoon I told my principal the story in case he had calls from parents about a teacher stripping in the classroom. Nothing was ever reported. It was never mentioned by the students or me.

Years later I ran into a young lady from that class. She was bringing me up-to-date on the students and things that had happened over the years. She started laughing and asked if I remembered the day my dress went up in the map (like I could forget it!). She said it was one of the funniest memories she had from elementary school, and she still chuckles when she thinks about it.

I am always amazed at the things for which teachers are remembered.

Linda Knowles

I Lost My Winnings in the First Grade

The summer before I accepted a first grade teaching position, I went to Tunica, Mississippi. Tunica is known for its casinos, and I was delighted that I won a whole bucketful of quarters. I brought my money back and kept the bucket of quarters on the top shelf of my closet, until . . . I lost my winnings in the first grade. How? Let me tell you my story.

For most of my teaching career, I taught older children or took part in the Title I program where I didn't have a regular classroom with its inherent responsibilities of collecting money or escorting students to restroom breaks, lunch, or recess. I had not been in charge of a classroom for six years so I was particularly concerned about this job since it involved these additional duties.

Even though I was a little anxious about this new assignment, I planned to give it my best shot. Three weeks before school started, I worked in my classroom daily to make it attractive and welcoming for my new students. My husband, John, helped me and we turned the classroom into a wonderful place for children.

The first day of school finally arrived. As I greeted my new students, they handed me boxes of kleenex, rolls of paper towels, containers of wipes, and cartons of markers, glue, crayons, and pencils. In no time at all, I was overwhelmed by this assortment of "stuff." Someone had failed to tell me that the kindergarten class last year had received a list of supplies to collect during the summer and bring on the first day of school.

In addition to this, each child was handing me money for lunch, fees, or snacks. The kids just smiled and said, "Here!" or "My mommy told me to give you this." And before I could ask the child's name, he was gone and another was handing me more money.

So there I stood on my first day of school in the middle of a pile of kleenex, toilet paper, paper towels, and construction paper, holding little wads of money from unknown origins and for unknown purposes.

I had no time to even think about where to put the supplies. I was too busy with my students. The kleenex came in handy to wipe noses and comfort those little darlings who cried and wanted to go home. I was also trying to talk to mamas who were worried about leaving their children at school with me. (I don't blame them; considering the confusion, I would have been worried too.)

Then snack time came. Each child insisted that he had paid me snack money. I looked at the unidentified money on my desk and thought that there must be a better way. That first day we all had snacks.

As my first lessons began, we hit another snag. I had distributed a few supplies to get us started, but each child wanted *his* own crayons or *his* own dry erase markers. "These aren't mine, Mrs. Kaiser. Mine had a red label on the outside." Or "I bought mine from K-Mart, Mrs. Kaiser; these are from Wal-Mart." I heard these comments over and over. The piles of supplies covered each corner of my room, and I saw no way of getting them returned this century to the rightful owners.

I decided to solve this problem quickly. "Children," I said, "the supplies you brought this morning were your donations for the *class*. We will *all* use them. They are no longer just yours. We will learn to share." I did such a good job with my "sharing" speech that one little boy, who was listening solemnly, clutched his lunch a little tighter and asked, "Is this lunch really just *mine*?"

For the next few mornings, I filled my pockets with quarters from the Tunica bucket in my closet before going to school. Until I could get a system working, I used them for snack or lunch money for cases I wasn't sure about. My winnings dwindled, but it was for a good cause. No one went hungry. My husband came every Monday morning to help with the money situation. It took John about two hours each session, but in time, we devised a workable system that I was able to handle myself.

Gradually things improved. In my 28 years of teaching, I know I never worked harder or spent so many hours in planning lessons and preparing for each day. My second year was better, for I began to feel like an experienced first grade teacher. I had my classroom routines and procedures set up, and the year went much smoother. I even had parents request that their children be placed in my room. We did lots of fun things that year. We put on a Thanksgiving play and had a huge Thanksgiving dinner with the kids making soup, cornbread, and festive table decorations. We also presented a Christmas program at the nursing home. I enjoyed the school year as much as the children did.

When I was going to school to get my degree, the young daughter of a friend of mine asked me what I wanted to be when I grew up. I have discovered that there is something exciting about working with children who are just beginning their educational experience, for you are so special in their lives. Now I am convinced that after all these years, I have found what I want to be when I grow up—*a first grade teacher!*

Martha Dyer Kaiser

The Best and the Brightest

Young people accomplish more in an environment that is supportive, caring, and encouraging. When individuals know others have high expectations of them, they usually rise to the occasion. The following story illustrates that there is a great deal of truth in the idea that "you get what you expect."

A first year teacher was assigned to a seventh grade classroom in a new middle school. During the first few weeks of the semester, the school system decided to administer a test, similar to an I.Q. test, to all seventh-graders.

A few days after the test was given, the assistant principal visited the class of the new teacher, Sandy Williams. Miss Williams was busy teaching her unit on map study. Her students were involved in constructing their own maps of the neighborhood, drawing in streets and buildings, and deciding the best routes to take between strategic locations. The assistant principal decided it would be best not to interrupt the lesson, so he only whispered to Miss

Williams as he left, "I'll put this note on your desk for you to look at later. It's some figures you'll need."

That afternoon Miss Williams was getting ready to go home when she noticed the paper left on her desk by the assistant principal. It was a list of her students' names along with accompanying numbers. Oh, my, these are the results of the test we just took, she thought. And look at how well my students scored!

She realized, on closer inspection, that no one in her class had an I.Q. lower than 110. Why, this is wonderful, she thought. My students are above average! She smiled as she said to herself, *I always knew they were smart!*

The next morning, Miss Williams was exuberant when she called her class to order. "Class, you scored so well on the test you took last week. I just want you to know how proud I am of you. There are no limits to what you'll be able to accomplish this year. You are among the best and the brightest in this school, and together, we're going to turn this school upside down by all we will achieve."

Her class beamed at receiving this praise and recognition. They began to see themselves in a new light.

During the next few weeks, energy radiated from Miss Williams' classroom. Everyone noticed it. Occasionally, the principal would steer visitors and supervisory personnel to her room, so they too could witness the high level of productivity taking place there. The students were working on independent projects and research papers. The room was alive with science and math corners and creative centers of every description. One could actually hear and feel learning taking place.

One afternoon Miss Williams ran into the assistant principal in the faculty lounge. "Thank you for showing me the I.Q. scores. I couldn't believe that my students were that bright!"

"What I.Q. scores? We didn't get any I.Q. scores," he replied. "In fact, after the kids took those tests, the system thought better of that decision and cancelled the whole thing."

"But that list of scores you gave me; you know, the day you came into my room and . . ."

"I'm not sure what you're referring to, Miss Williams. The only list I've given you lately was the list of numbers ranging from 110 to 140. Now whatever you do," he said, pointing his finger for emphasis, "don't lose that sheet of paper 'cause it's your master list for the new hall lockers we've ordered for your kids."

Tee Carr

What Didn't I Love About School?

Those cuties Dick and Jane. Distinguished portraits of Presidents Washington and Lincoln. *Black* blackboards. Even the pole to raise and lower the high windows during warm weather. Simply put, I adored everything about my elementary school years.

Some mornings the cries of a kindergartner or first-grader reluctant to leave his mother echo through our lower grade wing. I can't understand those feelings. I love my mother ever so much, but being a part of kindergarten is unbelievable!

Oh, the choices. What to do first? Visit the sand table with its endless building possibilities such as castles, roads, and various landforms; or the gingerbread house complete with baby dolls, curtains, iron, and ironing board; or perhaps check out the eggs that were warmly incubating? No! Not yet! I just had to get in line and impatiently wait my turn to go down the slide that was, amazingly enough, *inside* the classroom!

Play, play, play. That's what we did the entire morning. We played at getting along, sharing, taking turns, learning the alphabet, our names, and numbers. Mrs. Marler was incredibly sweet and patient. Little did I know that the seed of school had been planted firmly in the rich, fertile soil of my young spirit and soul.

Then came first grade. Not as colorful as kindergarten, but after all, this was the *real* thing. There were 36 of us sitting nicely in those straight rows of new desks. One day we were molding I-can't-remember-what out of modeling clay. Suddenly it was time to put our clay away and get ready for lunch. Only it wasn't that easy. I had some new, fresh clay and it was stuck all over my desk. How will I ever get it off? I know, I'll use the edge of my scissors and scrape off the clay.

"Susan!" my teacher called out. "What are you doing with your scissors?"

All I remember was looking up with those infamous scissors poised above my messy desk. My teacher was hurrying toward me. Then everything became a blur because I began crying uncontrollably. Between tears I blurted out that I was only trying to clean up, just as she had asked. My teacher was understanding and kind, but I learned one important lesson that day: Never use scissors to scrape off clay from a new desk.

How I dearly loved and revered my teachers. They could do no wrong in my eyes. I remember their voice tones, their expressions and hand gestures, and above all, their clothes. This was during the fifties and my teachers wore beautiful suits with matching high-heeled shoes. I especially think now of Miss Gates with her strawberry blond hair whose gold, brown, and tan suits seemed tailor-made for her. Several of my teachers favored dresses. I thought they were all so elegant.

With each year came new surprises and treasures: Our small spelling books with new and varied activities on each page. *Think and Do Workbooks* that accompanied our readers. The English textbook that made our class snicker when we had to show where to place the apostrophe in "hell." Poems to memorize in Mrs. Matusek's class which continue to resound in my heart as well a my head even now. Physical education classes on television. "Chapel all-sings" on Friday when we'd sing *Waltzing Matilda, All Through the Night,* and *Make New Friends* from our palm-sized singing books. But all of this came long before our saddening time.

Our young president was assassinated in the fall of our sixth grade year. Seeing our teacher, with her head down on her desk, was a sight indelibly etched in our memories. How proud I was that she trusted us enough to show and share her feelings. That tragedy pierced our age of loving comfort and confident assurance. So much for the easy, relaxed time the early sixties copied from the previous decade. It was now time to end our romp through childhood and, reluctantly, face the reality of the future.

In time we went our separate ways. Some of us attended the junior high school in the neighborhood; others went to private schools. A few of us were reunited once more in high school, and we realized what a strong and priceless bond we shared.

Whatever became of that delicate little seed that was so deliberately planted? It took root, flourished, and blossomed. I believe that my early, positive experiences in school and my endearing relationships with my teachers were the reasons I decided to devote my life to working with children.

Yes, I became a teacher.

Laurie Massey McCall

The Right Choice

My first year of teaching was a difficult yet rewarding one. In the beginning, I was scared to death. I had accepted a first grade teaching position, and although I had received great training to be a teacher, I often had moments when I felt as though I didn't know the first thing about what I was doing or about what little first graders needed. There were 25 inner-city children in my classroom and somehow, someway, I was supposed to teach them to read.

During the first weeks of school, my students and I spent our days getting to know one another and reviewing skills previously taught in kindergarten. Much of the time was focused on setting up classroom rules, routines, and procedures to make our day run smoother. Sometimes I thought several of my charges were "testing the rookie," but on the whole, and sometimes to my surprise, things were going quite well.

That year teachers on the first grade level decided to have all the students read one story a week. We planned to correlate everything we did in science, health, social studies, journal writing, and sometimes, even math, to that particular story to give it additional meaning. We further planned to have the entire class read the story aloud every day in hopes that the repetitiveness would help the children learn and remember the words.

At first this was a struggle, for the children faltered and stumbled over the words resulting in a cacophony of noise. I began to think that some of the children who seemed to be doing all right were only memorizing the story. However, we persisted and we began to make progress, even though it was usually at a snail's pace.

During our reading time we would discuss vocabulary words, predict what would happen next in the story, answer specific questions about the characters, and have fun acting out their various roles. Every day, however, we would continue to read the story aloud, my voice always resonating deeper and stronger than those of my students.

One morning, about a month into the school year, we were discussing the story I had introduced the day before. After a quick review of the four new vocabulary words, I said, "This is one of my favorite stories. Let's read it again today; only this time, read with a little more feeling."

After a moment or two, I noticed how well the children were reading. I began to lower my voice and continued lowering it until it couldn't be heard above the children's voices. I was amazed at what I was hearing.

My children were reading—*actually reading!* I stopped and listened to them as they continued on without me. As they ended the story, the children looked up at me and grinned with satisfaction as if to say, "There, we did it!" I know my face must have lit up with pride for them.

That was a critical moment in the early months of my career. That incident highlighted what teaching is all about—giving children the skills and confidence to move forward on their own. For the first time, I really felt like a teacher. As I looked around at my room full of little readers, I knew in my heart that I had chosen the right profession.

Wes Castle

On the Last Day of School

Father,
a quiet tension fills the room
on this last day of school.
I expected exuberance and rowdiness,
but that came yesterday,
when there was still one day to go.
Today the children are disturbingly subdued.
I am embarrassed at my own emotions;
I cannot look at the children directly.

The room is so blank.
Our desks are cleaned out.
The last traces of the party have been swept away.
The charts and posters are down for the summer.

So now we sit quietly,
too wrought even for songs and games,
and we wait for the bus to come.

I expect to see these children again, of course,
but it won't be the same.
They know it,
and I know it.

They will come around to see me,
jealous of the new class,
and I will look at a room of little strangers
and miss the familiar faces.

In time
the strangers will become friends.
But every class is different and special;
no new group of children will ever take the place
of the one leaving me today.

Lord,
I have worked hard,
and I have loved these children dearly.
In investing in their future
I have cast my bread upon the waters,
content that I will find it after many days.

Lord, I commend them into your hands.

Elspeth Campbell Murphy

Part II

STUDENTS

Children are our most valuable
natural resources.

Herbert Hoover
31st American President

We Believe in Children

We believe in children,
Little ones, big ones, thin ones, and chubby ones.
There is faith in their eyes, love in their touch,
And hope in their attitude.
We thrill with them at life's joys,
Bow with them in worship,
And hold them close in tragedy.

We believe in children,
The fragile dream of yesterday,
Life's radiant reality today,
And vibrant substance of tomorrow.
We believe in children, for wherever we go,
We find yesterday's children
Who were nurtured in love, truth, and beauty
At work trying to make this world
A better place for everyone.

Author Unknown

The First Day of School

This column could be entitled: Confessions of a child entering school for the first time who according to adults has "nothing to worry about."

My name is Donald and I don't know anything.

I have new underwear, a new sweater, a loose tooth and I didn't sleep last night. I am worried.

What if the school bus jerks after I get on and I lose my balance and my pants rip and everyone laughs?

What if I have to go to the bathroom before we get to school?

What if a bell rings and everyone goes in a door and a man yells, "Where do you belong?" and I don't know.

What if my shoestring comes untied and someone says, "Your shoestring is untied. We'll all watch while you tie it"?

What if the trays in the cafeteria are too high for me to reach?

What if the thermos lid on my soup is on too tight and, when I try to open it, it breaks?

What if my loose tooth wants to come out when we're supposed to have our heads down and be quiet?

What if teacher tells the class to go to the bathroom and I can't go?

What if I get hot and want to take my sweater off and someone steals it?

What if I splash water on my name tag and my name disappears and no one will know who I am?

What if they send us out to play and all the swings are taken? What do I do?

What if the wind blows all the important papers out of my hands that I'm supposed to take home?

What if they mispronounce my last name and everyone laughs?

What if my teacher doesn't make her D's like Mom taught me?

What if I spend the whole day without a friend?

What if the teacher gives a seat to everyone and I'm left over?

What if the windows in the bus steam up and I won't be able to tell when I get to my stop?

I'm just a little kid, but maybe I'm smarter than I think I am. At least I know better than to tell a five-year-old with a loose tooth who has never been out of the yard by himself before that he has "nothing to worry about."

Erma Bombeck

Three Letters from Teddy

Teddy's letter came today and now that I've read it, I will place it in my cedar chest with the other things that are important to my life.

"I wanted you to be the first to know."

I smiled as I read the words he had written and my heart swelled with a pride that I had no right to feel.

I have not seen Teddy Stallard since he was a student in my fifth-grade class, fifteen years ago. It was early in my career, and I had only been teaching for two years.

From the first day he stepped into my classroom, I disliked Teddy. Teachers (although everyone knows differently) are not supposed to have favorites in a class, but most especially are they not to show dislike for a child, any child.

Nevertheless, every year there are one or two children that one cannot help but be attached to, for teachers are human, and it is human nature to like bright, pretty, intelligent people, whether they are ten years old or twenty-five. And sometimes, not too often fortunately, there will be one or two students to whom the teacher just can't seem to relate.

I had thought myself quite capable of handling my personal feelings along that line until Teddy walked into my life. There wasn't a child I particularly liked that year, but Teddy was most assuredly one I disliked.

He was dirty. Not just occasionally, but all the time. His hair hung low over his ears and he actually had to hold it out of his eyes as he wrote his papers in class. (And this was before it was fashionable to do so!) Too, he had a peculiar odor about him which I could never identify.

His physical faults were many, and his intellect left a lot to be desired, also. By the end of the first week I knew he was hopelessly behind the others. Not only was he behind; he was just plain slow! I began to withdraw from him immediately.

Any teacher will tell you that it's more of a pleasure to teach a bright child. It is definitely more rewarding for one's ego. But any teacher worth her credentials can channel work to the bright child, keeping him challenged and learning while she puts her major effort on the slower ones. Any teacher *can* do this. Most teachers *do* it, but I *didn't*. Not that year.

In fact, I concentrated on my best students and let the others follow along as best they could. Ashamed as I am to admit it, I took perverse pleasure in using my red pen, and each time I came to Teddy's papers, the cross-marks (and there were many) were always a little larger and a little redder than necessary.

"Poor work!" I would write with a flourish.

While I did not actually ridicule the boy, my attitude was obviously quite apparent to the class, for he quickly became the class "goat," the outcast—the unlovable and the unloved.

He knew I didn't like him, but he didn't know why. Nor did I know—then or now—why I felt such an intense dislike for him. All I know is that he was a little boy no one cared about, and I made no effort in his behalf.

The days rolled by and we made it through the Fall Festival, the Thanksgiving holidays, and I continued marking happily with my red pens.

As the Christmas holidays approached, I knew that Teddy would never catch up in time to be promoted to the sixth-grade level. He would be a repeater.

To justify myself, I went to his cumulative folder from time to time. He had very low grades for the first four years, but no grade failure. How he had made it, I didn't know. I closed my mind to the personal remarks:

First grade: "Teddy shows promise by work and attitude, but has a poor home situation."

Second grade: "Teddy could do better. Mother terminally ill. He receives little help at home."

Third grade: "Teddy is a pleasant boy. Helpful, but too serious. Slow learner. Mother passed away end of the year."

Fourth grade: "Very slow, but well behaved. Father shows no interest."

Well, they passed him four times, but he will certainly repeat fifth grade! Do him good! I said to myself.

And then the last day before the holiday arrived. Our little tree on the reading table sported paper and popcorn chains. Many gifts were heaped underneath, waiting for the big moment.

Teachers always get several gifts at Christmas, but mine that year seemed bigger and more elaborate than ever. There was not a student who had not brought me one. Each unwrapping brought squeals of delight and the proud giver would receive effusive thank-you's.

His gift wasn't the last one I picked up; in fact it was in the middle of the pile. Its wrapping was a brown paper bag and he had colored Christmas trees and red bells all over it. It was stuck together with masking tape.

"For Miss Thompson—From Teddy" it read.

The group was completely silent and for the first time I felt conspicuous, embarrassed because they all stood watching me unwrap that gift.

As I removed the last bit of masking tape, two items fell to my desk. A gaudy rhinestone bracelet with several stones missing and a small bottle of dime-store cologne—half empty.

I could hear the snickers and whispers and I wasn't sure I could look at Teddy.

"Isn't this lovely?" I asked, placing the bracelet on my wrist. "Teddy, would you help me fasten it?"

He smiled shyly as he fixed the clasp and I held up my wrist for all of them to admire.

There were a few hesitant *ooh's* and *ahh's* but as I dabbed the cologne behind my ears, all the little girls lined up for a dab behind their ears.

I continued to open the gifts until I reached the bottom of the pile. We ate our refreshments and the bell rang.

The children filed out with shouts of "See you next year!" and "Merry Christmas!" but Teddy waited at his desk.

When they had all left, he walked towards me clutching his gift and books to his chest.

"You smell just like Mom," he said softly. "Her bracelet looks real pretty on you, too. I'm glad you liked it."

He left quickly and I locked the door, sat down

at my desk and wept, resolving to make up to Teddy what I had deliberately deprived him of—a teacher who cared.

I stayed every afternoon with Teddy from the end of the Christmas holidays until the last day of school. Sometimes we worked together. Sometimes he worked alone while I drew up lesson plans or graded papers.

Slowly but surely he caught up with the rest of the class. Gradually there was a definite upward curve in his grades.

He did not have to repeat the fifth grade. In fact his final averages were among the highest in the class, and although I knew he would be moving out of the state when school was out, I was not worried for him. Teddy had reached a level that would stand him in good stead the following year, no matter where he went. He had enjoyed a measure of success and as we were taught in our teacher training courses: "Success builds success."

I did not hear from Teddy until seven years later, when his first letter appeared in my mailbox.

Dear Miss Thompson,

I just wanted you to be the first to know.
I will be graduating second in my class next month.

Very truly yours,
Teddy Stallard

I sent him a card of congratulations and a small package, a pen and pencil gift set. I wondered what he would do after graduation.

Four years later, Teddy's second letter came.

Dear Miss Thompson,

I wanted you to be the first to know. I was just informed that I'll be graduating first in my class. The university has not been easy, but I liked it.

Very truly yours,
Teddy Stallard

I sent him a good pair of sterling silver monogrammed cuff links and a card, so proud of him I could burst!

And now—today—Teddy's third letter.

Dear Miss Thompson,

I wanted you to be the first to know. As of today I am Theodore J. Stallard, MD. How about that!!??

I'm going to be married in July, the twenty-seventh, to be exact. I wanted to ask if you could come and sit where Mom would sit if she were here. I'll have no family there as Dad died last year.

Very truly yours,
Teddy Stallard

I'm not sure what kind of gift one sends to a doctor on completion of medical school and state boards. Maybe I'll just wait and take a wedding gift, but my note can't wait.

> Dear Ted,
> Congratulations! You made it and you did it yourself! In spite of those like me and not because of us, this day has come for you.
> God bless you. I'll be at that wedding with bells on!

> *Elizabeth Silance Ballard*

The Mural

I was a first year teacher and extremely happy to have secured a position teaching the fourth grade in a small country school. My principal asked me to have my class decorate the wall in the entrance hall just outside his office for the month of December.

Just after the Thanksgiving holidays my class began to plan a Christmas mural. We formed committees and the children set about to select the part of the project they wanted as their own.

Mike and Randy wanted to make the stars. These two boys had been the terror of the school since they entered first grade, always in some kind of trouble, never really connecting with anyone or anything. With a great deal of trepidation, but tempered with hope and trust, I hesitantly assigned Mike and Randy "the stars." To my amazement, the boys threw themselves into this project. They spent every extra minute drawing, cutting out, and coloring their stars. They ended up with about a dozen different shapes of various sizes which somewhat resembled stars in that they all were yellow and had five points.

The following week our entire class spent a joyous morning arranging our Christmas scene in the entrance hall. Mike and Randy carefully pinned their odd shaped creations to strategic positions on the blue sky. Upon completion, however, one could tell that this fourth grade class had more enthusiasm than talent.

A few days later I was standing in the hall, lining up the class for lunch. Suddenly Mike and Randy stepped out of line and walked over to the Christmas mural. They stared at the scene and even took a few steps back to get a better view. Then I heard Randy say quietly but with sincere pride, "Looka there, Mike, them's our stars. Ain't they beautiful!" Tears of joy filled my eyes as I looked at these two boys admiring their work. I can still hear those words thirty years later.

Frances P. Buttolph

Six Forever

This is the story of Kimberly, a first-grader I had in class several years ago. Kimberly touched me in a very special way and became a part of me I'll remember forever.

It all began in August a few weeks before school started when I attended an out-of-town professional inservice day. It turned out to be one of those wonderful days, full of exciting and useful ideas for teaching young children. An educator who had traveled in Australia hosted one of the sessions on language development I attended. While I don't remember her name, I still use the idea from "down under" she gave us that day.

She suggested that to increase language skills in our young charges, we should have our students collect poems and songs beginning the first day of school. This approach could include various skills, and it would only be limited by our lack of imagination. When I started my first grade class that fall, I gave each child a folder labeled *Poem and Song Book,* and we began to collect timely verses.

A few weeks into the year when we began to work on number words, I remembered one poem quite vividly. It had the number words from one to six and was simple and charming. However, I hadn't written it down, I did not remember the author's name, and all I had to go on was the first line and the gist of the thing. I began to look through books, ask colleagues, and generally make a nuisance of myself looking for the poem. Finally someone suggested that the author might be A. A. Milne. I found the poem and taught it to my children:

The End

When I was One,

I had just begun.

When I was Two,

I was nearly new.

When I was Three,

I was hardly Me.

When I was Four,

I was not much more.

When I was Five,

I was just alive.

But now I am Six, I'm as clever as clever.

So I think I'll be six now forever and ever.

We made a big poster with removable word cards for the number words and were quickly able to recognize these. The children loved this poem and their little books, and they were often seen getting them out and reciting the poems and singing the songs.

My class that year included a beautiful little girl with deep brown eyes and thick black curls. She was new to our school. When I read her registration information, I noted the medical section that stated "heart problems." The mother assured me that while she might tire more easily than the other children, there were no special precautions I needed to take with Kimberly.

Kimberly was such a bright and eager little first-grader. She loved books and just seemed to soak up any lesson given to her. She especially loved the poems and songs we learned that fall. As the days went by, I began to notice that she did indeed tire quickly. On the playground, she would run around with the other little girls for awhile and then would often come sit quietly by me and watch the antics of her classmates. As the warm days of late summer gave way to the cooler days of fall, it seemed that more and more often Kimberly would be so worn out after a few minutes of play that I would end up carrying her back to the classroom. On these days, we would call her mom who always came promptly and took her home to rest.

During this time I learned that Kimberly had one heart surgery to try to correct a serious birth defect and that another surgery would be necessary if she was to lead a normal life. She seemed to miss more and more school days and be at a very low ebb the days she did come. Finally around Thanksgiving, her mom told me that the doctors wanted to perform Kimberly's surgery during Christmas break. Her mom seemed so optimistic that I never realized the seriousness of the problem. The doctor wanted Kimberly to stay home to guard against colds and such that little ones usually share, so her mom came to the school daily to get her work.

Kimberly was poked and prodded and tested often in those days before the surgery. Just before Christmas, her mom brought her in with some cookies for the class that they had baked together. I wanted to give her a big hug but I could see that she had lost weight and was moving slowly—sore from all the testing—so I gave her a light squeeze and a big smile as she left our classroom.

Two days after Christmas, Kimberly's mom called me at home to tell me that Kimberly had died in the recovery room. Although the surgery was a success, her heart just wasn't strong enough to keep going. At the funeral home, Kimberly's mother shared with me how much her daughter had loved school and reading. She told me how her other children had looked through Kimberly's things and found the *Poem and Song Book*. They showed her the poem I had searched for so diligently and told their mother that it was Kimberly's favorite.

At the funeral, the first thing the minister did was to read that poem. I sat there stunned, because it *was* Kimberly! Kimberly loved living and learning, and had the simple faith that only a child can. Her mother said that Kimberly told her on the way to the hospital that if she didn't wake up from the surgery, she'd wait for her mother in heaven. She told her mother not to worry if it was crowded because she'd be waiting inside, behind the gate.

And so she is six. She is as clever as clever. And she will be six now, for ever and ever.

The next year our new literature-based reading series had that dear poem at the end of one of the anthologies. It took me several years to be able to recite it again to a class and to use the poster with the removable number words. I finally made myself use it. Now, whenever I do, I picture Kimberly reciting the poem as she waits behind the gate for the rest of us.

Linda Green Johnson

Food for Thought

My fourth-graders' lunch period had ended, and as usual, there sat my two regulars who never finished their lunch in the allotted time. Each day as their classmates were returning trays and getting in line, these two had figured out to the exact number of seconds how they could be last in line.

On this particular day, one of the two, Melvin, seemed to be rushing to complete his lunch. As we were about to leave the cafeteria, I spotted an unusual object that appeared to be wet in Melvin's back pocket. When I approached him, I motioned to his pocket and asked if he was taking some of his lunch out of the cafeteria.

"Yes, Ma'am, it's my fudgesicle," he replied.

"And what are you planning to do with it?"

"Oh," he said, with great assurance, "I'm saving it to eat this afternoon at recess."

Jackie Elkins

Harv Was Just Lucky

In 1940 we moved to Kentucky. I was put in grade 3A at my new school. It operated on the semester system, so successful completion of 3A work moved you to 3B.

Most of the students were not memorable, but one boy sticks in my mind today, 60 years later. I will call him Harvey (not his real name). I first saw him on my first day of school when I was shown to the standard student armchair desk.

He was sitting on a wide bench in the rear of the classroom. A library table was in front of him, serving as his desk. He probably weighed 300 pounds even then. He had the homemade "bowl" haircut affected by poor families who couldn't afford the store-bought cut with a full thatch on top and white sidewalls.

Winter or summer, he wore Blue Bell overalls, unbuttoned at the sidesplit to give him more room. In the winter he wore heavy shirts; in the summer, a light loose shirt. He wore "Boondocker" shoes—the kind you lace up to the ankles—with a steel toe. They lasted forever and served one well in the neighborhood football games. A missed tackle and a steel toe to the forehead would give one a new respect for the ball carrier.

Regarding the size contrast between Harvey and the rest of us, I probably weighed between 50 and 60 pounds, about the average size then for an eight-year old. Most of us dressed somewhat like Harv. It was post-depression, but times were still hard. We didn't feel poor though, because none of us had any money. You are only poor if others have something and you don't.

I lived in "The Bottom," hemmed in between the river and the train tracks. Harv lived down the creek road. In my section there were about 35-40 boys of elementary and junior high age. And there was an education standard in "The Bottom." If you made all A's, chances are you would live hard and be called *Brown Nose*. If you flunked, you would be greeted derisively as *Dumbbell.* So the way to get along was to get C's and D's. When you were asked how you did at semester's end, the politically correct answer was, "I passed." You didn't want your grades to be too good or too bad.

Harv was a loner. We'd see him walking along the tracks once in a while, picking up bits of wire, rags, or bottles. While he read aloud quite proficiently in class, he had nothing to say socially. But no one messed with him or made fun of him. An often voiced fear was the possibility that Harv would get mad at you and sit on you, effectively squeezing you to death.

When I was promoted to 3B, Harv stayed in 3A. He didn't pass, but no one said anything to him. In fact, Harv didn't make it to 3B until I was in 4B. Ultimately, I made it to 6B and was promoted to junior high school. I think Harv was in 5A then. I lost track of his scholastic progress when I went to junior high, but we'd see him ambling down the tracks, picking up junk. Harv turned 16 when he was in 6B. At age 16, you could legally quit school. He did.

You could also get a driver's license at 16, and it wasn't long before we started to see Harv putt-putting around in an old Model T Ford. He had cut off the back of the cab and fashioned it into a small truck bed. By this time he was so huge he looked like an adult sitting on one of those children's cars, literally stuffed into that small cab, Blue Bells blowing in the breeze. Harv remained a loner. I guess he weighed close to 500 pounds by then.

I moved away, grew up, and didn't get back to the hometown for several years. While riding around the town one day with my buddies and catching up on old times, my friend Paul pointed out an ostentatious house with huge Greek columns on a large rolling estate.

"Bet you don't know who lives there," Paul said.

Of course I didn't.

"Harv lives there. He's still huge, but he's got a wife and six kids, owns the biggest junkyard in the tri-state area, and is worth millions of dollars. He gives money to all the charities. He's a real big shot now! He's on all the local boards and no politician in this town makes a move without Harv's okay."

Kids by nature are insensitive, but now that I was grown, I felt sort of good knowing Harv had achieved success. I'd always felt sad when I'd thought of him.

Later, I reflected on this phenomenon. How did a guy who didn't finish 6B end up so successful? Let's see, to get to 6B, he had to be able to give written and oral book reports, know the parts of a sentence and be able to diagram them, read several classics, and write letters with the proper salutation, punctuation, and close.

He had to know addition, subtraction, multiplication, long division, decimals, beginning algebra, geography, and the social sciences. Come to think of it, by the time he'd passed all the work through 6A, he knew just about everything he had to know to become a successful businessman.

But Harv had some luck too. He was lucky enough to be born and educated during the depression and post-depression years. He was lucky there was no social promotion at that time. If a student didn't know the work, he sat there until he did. So he learned what he had to know to make it in the world of business.

He was lucky there were no individuals or institutions to focus on his obesity and social problems and sidetrack him by refocusing on his personal problems. They would only have directed him to wallow in self-pity rather than do his schoolwork and life's work.

He was lucky no one was there to coddle him or let him off the hook. He had to deal with the pragmatics of life.

It's too bad that many of the kids today aren't as lucky as Harv.

Herb Criswell

Aside from That, Mrs. Jones . . .

Kerry was an energetic, freckled-faced, eleven-year-old who was a member of my exceptional education class. She had missed school several times during the year because she had a series of eye surgeries. In the end she lost her eye, and the doctor replaced it with an artificial one. Upon returning to school, Kerry was delighted to hear that the children in her room thought she looked fantastic.

Spurred on by the positive comments of her classmates, Kerry was eager to show off her new look to the students in the regular education classes. Thirty minutes after she left my class, one of the students ran into my room and called out to me, "Mrs. Jones, come quick! Kerry's eye fell out!" I dashed to the classroom and escorted Kerry out. We washed the eye, calmly put it back in, and we both resumed our schedules.

That afternoon, I stopped by the office to pick up my messages. The school secretary spoke to me and asked, "How are things going today, Mrs. Jones?" I watched her mouth drop open as I replied, "Other than Kerry's eye falling out, it's been a pretty good day!"

Connie Jones

Cipher in the Snow

It started with tragedy on a biting cold February morning. I was driving behind the Milford Corners bus as I did most snowy mornings on my way to school. It veered and stopped short at the hotel, which it had no business doing, and I was annoyed as I had to come to an unexpected stop. A boy lurched out of the bus, reeled, stumbled, and collapsed on the snow bank at the curb. The bus driver and I reached him at the same moment. His thin, hollow face was white even against the snow.

"He's dead," the driver whispered.

It didn't register for a minute. I glanced quickly at the scared young faces staring down at us from the school bus. "A doctor! Quick! I'll phone from the hotel. . . ."

"No use. I tell you, he's dead." The driver looked down at the boy's still form. "He never even said he felt bad," he muttered, "just tapped me on the shoulder and said, real quiet, 'I'm sorry. I have to get off at the hotel.' That's all. Polite and apologizing like."

At school, the giggling, shuffling morning noise quieted as the news went down the halls. I passed a huddle of girls. "Who was it? Who dropped dead on the way to school?" I heard one of them half-whisper.

"Don't know his name; some kid from Milford Corners," was the reply.

It was like that in the faculty room and the principal's office. "I'd appreciate you going out to tell the parents," the principal told me. "They haven't a phone and anyway, somebody from school should go there in person. I'll cover your classes."

"Why me?" I asked. "Wouldn't it be better if you did it?"

"I didn't know the boy," the principal admitted levelly. "And in last year's sophomore personalities column, I noticed that you were listed as his favorite teacher."

I drove through the snow and cold down the bad canyon road to the Evans' place and thought about the boy, Cliff Evans. His favorite teacher! Why, he hasn't spoken two words to me in two years! I could see him in my mind's eye all right, sitting back there in the last seat in my afternoon literature class. He came in the room by himself and left by himself. "Cliff Evans," I muttered to myself, "a boy who never talked." I thought a minute. "A boy who never smiled. I never saw him smile once."

The big ranch kitchen was clean and warm. I blurted out my news somehow. Mrs. Evans reached blindly toward a chair. "He never said anything about bein' ailing."

His stepfather snorted. "He ain't said nothin' about anything since I moved in here."

Mrs. Evans pushed a pan to the back of the stove and began to untie her apron. "Now hold on," her husband snapped. "I got to have breakfast before I go to town. Nothin' we can do now anyway. If Cliff hadn't been so dumb, he'd have told us he didn't feel good."

After school I sat in the office and stared bleakly at the records spread out before me. I was to close the file and write his obituary for the school paper. The almost bare sheets mocked the effort. Cliff Evans, white, never legally adopted by stepfather, five young half-brothers and sisters. These meager strands of information and the list of D grades were all the records had to offer.

Cliff Evans had silently come in the school door in the mornings and gone out the school door in the evenings, and that was all. He had never belonged to a club. He had never played on a team. He had never held an office. As far as I could tell, he had never done one happy, noisy kid thing. He had never been anybody at all.

How do you go about making a boy into a zero? The grade school records showed me much of the answer. The first and second grade teachers' annotations read "sweet, shy child; timid but eager." Then the third grade note had opened the attack. Some teacher had written in a good, firm hand, "Cliff won't talk. Uncooperative. Slow learner." The other academic sheep had followed with *dull, slow-witted, low I.Q.* They became correct. The boy's I.Q. score in the ninth grade was listed at 83. But his I.Q. in the third grade had been 106. The score didn't go under 100 until the seventh grade. Even shy, timid, sweet children have resilience. It takes time to break them.

I stomped to the typewriter and wrote a savage report pointing out what education had done to Cliff Evans. I slapped a copy on the principal's desk and another in the sad, dog-eared file. I slammed the file and crashed the office door shut as I left for home. But I didn't feel much better. A little boy kept walking after me, a boy with a peaked face, a skinny body in faded jeans, and big eyes that had searched for a long time and then had become veiled.

I could guess how many times he'd been chosen last to be on a team, how many whispered child conversations had excluded him, how many times he hadn't been asked. I could see the faces and hear the voices that said over and over, "You're dumb. You're dumb. You're just a nothing, Cliff Evans."

A child is a believing creature. Cliff undoubtedly believed them. Suddenly it seemed clear to me: When finally there was nothing left at all for Cliff Evans, he collapsed on a snow bank and went away. The doctor might list "heart failure" as the cause of death, but that wouldn't change my mind.

We couldn't find ten students in the school who had known Cliff well enough to attend the funeral as his friends. So the student body officers and a committee from the junior class went as a group to the church, being politely sad. I attended the services with them, and sat through it with a lump of cold lead in my chest and a big resolve growing in me.

I've never forgotten Cliff Evans or that resolve. He has been my challenge year after year, class after class. I look up and down the rows carefully each September at the unfamiliar faces. I look for veiled eyes or bodies slumped into a seat in an alien world. "Look, kids," I say silently, "I may not do anything else for you this year, but not one of you is going to come out of here a nobody. I'll work or fight to the bitter end doing battle with anyone or anything, but I won't have one of you coming out of here thinking himself a zero."

Most of the time—not always, but *most* of the time—I've succeeded.

Jean Mizer Todhunter

Get a Life!

Some of the more hilarious moments in my long tenure as an elementary school principal occurred during visits and conversations with kindergarten children.

One I shall never forget happened on the first day of the school year, an hour or so after the day began, when I decided to visit the kindergarten classes. I always made it a priority to be highly visible on the first days of school so the children would become familiar with their principal.

Almost immediately upon entering the kindergarten classroom and before the teacher could introduce me to her children, one little fellow in the class inched his way up to me and asked, "Why are you still hanging 'round here? *My* daddy works!"

Darwin Lane

Jake, the Lost One

In 1976 I became a teaching principal in an elementary school in a rural county in Tennessee. The school is located in an isolated but breathtakingly beautiful community that is geographically situated so that it really doesn't seem to belong to either Tennessee or Georgia, the two states it borders. The people living there were some of the finest I have ever encountered in my teaching career, deeply caring about their children's education and the one school which provided that opportunity for them.

This is where I met Jake, one of the few unloved outcasts of the community. In my mind he quickly became the Huckleberry Finn of my existence; and by default, since no one else really wanted to deal with him, he became my shadow at the school. From second grade until he left the school at the end of sixth grade, he was in my classroom more than anyone else's, because my room was where the discipline problems were sent.

Jake was the roughest, toughest, and meanest bully anyone ever encountered. His hair was never combed or cut, his teeth badly needed braces, and he was overweight. He walked with a marked limp because he refused to stop wading in the creek when he was placed in a cast for a broken leg which, of course, healed incorrectly. Because Jake's mother had been committed to the state asylum for the insane where he was conceived, Jake was sent back home to live with elderly grandparents who could only provide for his most basic needs of food and shelter.

His home near the mountain had a dirt floor with tarpaper windows and could only be reached by scaling a fairly formidable rock wall. I discovered all of this while taking him home one day after a suspension from school that he received for hitting me. Not only had I suspended him, but I had hit him back because he needed to know I cared enough not to be afraid of him. After taking him to his home and seeing the conditions there, I tearfully returned him to school. I never sent him there again for punishment no matter how bad his behavior became.

By the time Jake reached sixth grade, it was obvious that he had developed some criminal tendencies. All of the patience and intervention we had to offer at the school could not alleviate the pain or remediate the deficiencies of his life. I began to doubt that he would survive the first month of school in the seventh grade at a middle school he would be attending fifteen miles away at the county seat. I knew the school was too big and the staff too small to begin to address Jake's needs. Jake was actually able to make it through several months of middle school before dropping out. He had been suspended many times, so he really did not spend enough time at school to do a lot of damage to himself or others while he was there. I am sure the school system counted its blessings in this category, and after the last suspension, the school did not invite him back.

Having a tremendous amount of time on his hands was not to Jake's advantage, and it was not long before he began setting fires for the fun of it. His misbehavior escalated, and one fateful Thanksgiving weekend, Jake committed a capital crime. Since there were eyewitnesses, he was quickly arrested and subsequently convicted. He was nineteen years old at the time. I read the account of the crime, trial, and life sentencing in the newspaper. I thought about my days with Jake and began to analyze each day I had spent with him. My inadequacy in helping him distressed me deeply.

Years later I was at home one evening helping my own children with their homework when I received a phone call from the state penitentiary. The person on the other end of the line was a staff psychiatrist for the prison. She was a woman that in conversation impressed me as being rather hardened by her job, but she matter-of-factly told me she was working with an inmate she referred to as "Potter" whom she could not get off her mind. Her exact words to me were, "The look on this man's face haunts me."

She was treating him for severe depression that had resulted in an attempted suicide, and she was having little success getting any response from him. She feared he was not going to survive much more of his life sentence. She had tracked me with information he had given her. According to the psychiatrist, I was the only person he would discuss with her. From what she could ascertain, I was probably the one person in his life who had offered him any of the love, affection, or support he had needed. He said I was the only person that ever "liked" him or "stayed."

She did not ask me for help but indicated that she would tell him that we had talked; and I, of course, sent some feeble words of encouragement. I believe the doctor just needed to talk to another human being who might know or care about her patient.

I considered writing or visiting Jake, but I was not strong enough emotionally to do it. I can honestly say, however, that not many days go by without my mind reflecting on this child that I had within my power to influence for a small part of his life.

Whenever a student is driving me crazy or I have a particularly disappointing week, I think of Jake. I can then put it all in true perspective. I might just again be that one person who can make a lasting impression with a smile, a touch, or perhaps some real commitment and trust. There is always the possibility that instead of being lost like Jake, the next student might respond differently and be saved from a horrible fate.

I also take some small comfort in the fact that in his darkest hour, he could remember one glimmer of kindness and had seen one example of the goodness in human nature. I am glad that as a child he at least felt someone thought he was special.

I have come to accept the truth that as a teacher I really do have the capacity to shape and influence lives, and that even though I can't "win them all," I must honor his wretched life with the determination to never give up trying. Because Jake crossed the path of my life, I now understand this job of teaching can be the most profoundly important profession in the world.

Sharon Richards Vaughn

Oh, No! It's You Again!

In my second year of teaching, I had 34 fourth-graders. Among them was a mischievous student of average ability by the name of Jerry Anderson. Although he was quite often the class clown, Jerry was a likeable student, so we fared quite well.

The next year, Davenport Elementary School opened, and I was reassigned there to teach a split fourth and fifth grade combination classroom. Who was in my class but Jerry! He had moved to that area over the summer and didn't know many students. I, too, didn't know many people since most of the teachers, like me, had come from other schools. So Jerry and I were glad to see each other.

The next year I was assigned to teach sixth grade, and there was Jerry again. He had a great big grin on his face when he entered the classroom and saw a familiar face at the front of the room.

The following year Alton Park Junior High School opened, and the principal selected me as one of the teachers to accompany him to the new school. I taught seventh grade students in a language arts and social studies block. When the second group of students entered my classroom that first morning, I was delighted to see a friendly face. Jerry looked at me rather surprisingly and asked, "Are you going to be my teacher *forever?*"

Thirty years later, Jerry and I met again at a church gathering. He was there with his beautiful wife and daughter, and he announced that he was the associate pastor at that church. We were truly happy to see each other after all those years. Later he stood before the congregation to speak. It was a special moment for me when Jerry, filled with emotion, introduced me to the group and declared that I was *always* his favorite teacher.

Jewell Baldwin Cousin

Michael

When Michael entered my Freshman Seminar class for the first time, I was taken by the little-boy, almost angelic face framed by tousled blond curls and accented by a slightly dimpled chin. He smiled faintly, but I detected a sadness in his brown eyes that troubled me. He sat, usually, with his chin resting on hands that lay across the top of his desk, and he seldom spoke in class discussion or even to those students close around him.

But he listened.

He listened as we studied Maslow's Basic Human Needs and the difference between internal and external self-esteem. He listened as we described the types of masks we all wear to protect our real selves and to hide our own vulnerabilities. He listened as we discussed relationships and how to deal with disappointment, and the pain that can sometimes be caused by the ones we love the most. He listened when we concluded that we cannot change what has happened to us; we can only change our response to what has happened.

Soon he began to add occasional comments—comments that reflected deep thought and understanding—comments that came from the heart.

And then his classmates listened.

Sometimes he stayed after class to talk with me briefly. As time passed, I noted that he began to sit up straighter and smile more often—and the smile was genuine.

At the end of the semester when the students walked out of my classroom for the last time, each of them hugged me, including Michael. I walked back to my desk, reflecting on the time we had spent together and wondering which of the things we had studied they might carry with them as they progressed through their years in high school and on into adulthood. There, beside my textbook, lay a note written on crumpled notebook paper but neatly folded. I opened it and read:

Dear Mrs. Honeycutt,

I have enjoyed being in your class. The things we have studied and the things you have said have kept me from taking my life.

Thank you.

Love,
Michael

In my thirty-one years of teaching, this experience with Michael stands as my greatest reward. Not anyone or anything has shown me more what a powerful impact a teacher can have on the lives of her students.

Vickie Honeycutt

The Letter

Friday, September 17, 1999
A Promise to Myself   Time 4:06

A simple heading on a folded page of notebook paper handed to me without ceremony as I began a daily classroom ritual—getting our minds right. "Our minds" because I must include myself. My twenty students and I try to focus our concentration on the lessons ahead.

After a half-hour of math problems and another half-hour of basic grammar, we ease into a period of working individually in folders. I move about the room and sit next to each inmate to check and initial "homework."

I unfolded the paper and pressed it into his notebook with care, befitting what amounted to a document—a milestone in the life of a man who measures time in years: "Last night I gave my life to Jesus Christ—Thursday night around 9 o'clock . . ."

I spent the allotted five minutes with him correcting his mistakes on this special letter (everything—no exceptions—must be corrected in this class, for after all, isn't this called a *correctional* institution?). At the bottom of his paper, I wrote the comment, "Steve, I'm very proud of you."

He would leave class that afternoon to return to a cell he shares with two other men in a cellblock containing two hundred and fifty prisoners of a total population of over seventeen hundred.

He will leave in a few months and will live with his mother. His son is in another prison in another state.

Thirty-six-year-old Steve spent his last twelve years in three separate prisons because he could not control himself. He has worked very hard this year to manage his temper. Perhaps he is ready to leave.

The last line in his letter touches me: "I have a friend in prison who helps me the way I need to go—a brother, a good brother."

I wonder what will happen to him.

Pete Carnes

What It Means to Teach

I began my teaching career as a physical education teacher. That first year was a tremendous blessing for me, given the fact that I was able to work with so many wonderful and bright children. I suppose there were a couple of students I couldn't reach or didn't connect with, but for the most part, I believe I touched students' lives in a positive way, as they did mine.

There was one student that I will never forget. Her name was Laura and it was her first year at the school. Each time her kindergarten class came to the gym was a special time for me. The kids were cute, sweet, and eager to learn. Laura quickly found a special place in my heart. I can't put a finger on exactly *why*, but from Day One I developed a unique bond with her.

Laura usually came to school happy, full of energy, and talkative. One day, however, I saw her in the hall with an unhappy look on her face so I asked her what was the matter. She simply said, "I'm having a bad day." Well, her bad day extended to a bad week. It was breaking my heart to see this little girl so sad.

One morning I saw Laura's mother taking her to class so I decided to inquire as to what was bothering Laura. I introduced myself, and she told me Laura often talked about me and always looked forward to my class. As tears formed in her eyes, Laura's mother whispered that she and her husband were having some family problems at home but progress was being made. It upset me to think that her little girl might be affected by a broken home like so many of today's kids experience. I assured Laura's mother that I would do whatever I could to keep Laura happy at school.

Eventually things began to improve for Laura. After a few months, she was once again smiling and acting like she didn't have a care in the world. Each day I took a moment to see how she was doing or give her a smile, a high-five, or a word of encouragement.

The school year seemed to fly by and before I knew it, the year came to a close. The last day was hectic because we had so many activities taking place. As I said farewell to my fifth grade students, I noticed it was almost time for the final bell to ring. There was no way I'd miss saying goodbye to Laura. When I got to her room, I found her busily gathering her things. Laura's mother was there, too, and suddenly her face lit up and she smiled, explaining that she and her husband had settled their differences and things were going well. What a relief it was to hear that. I'll never forget what came next. She looked me straight in the eyes and said, "Thank you so much for taking a special interest in my daughter." Those simple words meant so much to me, and they still do.

As I watched Laura walk away smiling and laughing, holding her mother's hand, it made me proud to be a teacher. I will never take the title of teacher for granted. We are responsible for teaching various skills and lessons, but we are also responsible for meeting the emotional needs of our children and for being there when they need us. Laura may not remember me very well one day, but I know I will never forget that little girl who captured a piece of my heart.

Jeff Scott

A Special Gift

My last day of work! At 4 o'clock this afternoon, I'll join the ranks of the retired. My career as a principal will be over. No more bus problems or fund-raisers. No more paperwork, deadlines, conflicts, or Monday morning stress. No more fighting freeway rush hours and arriving at home long after dark.

Just think about it. I'll have time to soak for hours in a hot tub filled with bubble bath. And I can stay up past midnight and watch a late movie and not worry about having to get up and go to work the next day. If I want to, I can sleep until ten. And I can have a real breakfast with two cups of steaming coffee. Maybe three.

I will miss the kids terribly. I can't imagine what it will be like not to be surrounded by their lively conversations, laughter, and squeezing hugs. What will I do without their corny Valentines and genuine love notes left on my desk? But I don't want to think about that now. This is supposed to be a happy day. After all, I'm retiring! I'm beginning a new life.

"Good Morning, Tee," said Jackie, the school secretary. "How are you this morning?"

"I'm fine, Jackie. Really, I am," I replied, as I busied myself emptying out my desk.

"Are you sure?" she inquired as her eyes followed me. "I still can't believe this is really your last day."

"Jackie, don't get me started! I've made up my mind not to be sad today, not to cry."

Jackie had been a school secretary for over ten years, beginning with me at the first school where I was a new principal. Later, when I transferred to this larger school, I requested that she accompany me. We had worked so closely that she probably knew me better than anyone else.

Just then Mrs. Patten, a second grade teacher, entered the office followed by two little giggly girls holding their hands behind their backs.

"Dr. Carr, two of my students, Angie and Latisha, need to see you this morning. I told them to wait until a little later but they insisted that they see you now. Do you have a minute?" she asked.

"Of course, Mrs. Patten," I replied. "Girls, what seems to be the problem?"

"No problem, Dr. Carr," replied Latisha. "We know this is your last day today, and you won't be our principal next year."

"That's right, girls, but I'm sure your next principal will be very nice," I said, reassuring them, thinking they were concerned about who would take my place.

"Well, Dr. Carr, we just wanted to tell you we'll miss you, and we wanted to give you a goodbye present," said Angie.

"But we didn't have any money," stated Latisha, sadly, as she shrugged her shoulders in frustration.

"Girls," I said, "that's a beautiful thought, but you don't need to give me a gift. I do appreciate your thinking of me, but I don't want you spending money on me."

"Well, Dr. Carr, we didn't need any money 'cause after we thought and thought about it, we came up with something real good for you," said Angie.

"And it didn't cost us anything!" stated Latisha, grinning from ear to ear. "Not a penny!"

The two girls brought their hands from behind their backs. They were each holding a well-worn teddy bear, one brown and one honey colored.

"Here, Dr. Carr, these are for you!" they said in unison.

"I . . .uh . . ." I stammered.

"These are our favorite teddy bears," Latisha stated. "We've had them forever."

"They're our special presents for you," Angie said, beaming with pride.

Both girls held up their gifts for me to take.

"But, girls . . ." I said, trying to find the words to

tell them that I couldn't take their most treasured possessions.

"Oh, Dr. Carr," Jackie exclaimed, sensing my problem and coming to my rescue, "aren't these girls wonderful! What a super gift!" Jackie's eyes told me what I should do. Sometimes it is better to graciously receive than to give.

I took the bears and said, "Angie, Latisha, I am so honored that you want to give me your very own teddy bears. I can see how much you have loved them."

Much of the brown fur of one bear had been rubbed off. And the other one's right ear was dangling, badly in need of repair. But the little bear faces looked up at me with expressions that seemed to say they were proud to have been loved so much by these dear children.

"We sleep with them every night, Dr. Carr. But that's O.K. We want you to have them so you won't forget us," said Latisha.

I knelt down, drew the girls to me, and gave them a big hug. And suddenly the tears came—both theirs and mine. The three of us remained there holding each other with the two bears pressed tightly between us. I looked up and saw Jackie wiping her eyes. Mrs. Patten was teary-eyed too.

And it was O.K. to cry. In fact, it felt good.

That afternoon my faculty gave me a farewell party and when all the best wishes, goodbyes, and promises to keep in touch had been said, I drove home. The two bears rode beside me in the passenger seat.

That night I made the bears a home on my desk, right between my well-worn Webster's Dictionary and my over-zealous philodendron. They remained there and kept me company during the following years when I added a computer and printer to my desk and began writing books for and about teachers.

There were times when I looked back over my life as a teacher and principal and wondered if I had done all that I could to exert a positive influence on my students and show I really cared about them. I guess all teachers want to be reassured that they did their best to shape and lead their students. But I had only to glance at my two straggly, still somewhat-furry guardians propped on my desk and steadfastly watching over me to remember and cherish the special bond that exists between teachers and children. If we can become as permanently love-worn from this unique relationship as the teddies have, then all have benefited.

Tee Carr

Part III

TEACHERS

One looks back with appreciation to the brilliant teachers, but with gratitude to those who touched our human feelings.

Carl Jung
Swiss Psychologist

What Are Teachers Made Of?

Teachers are made of laughter, gold stars, smiley faces, Happy Grams, and good notes written to Moms.

They are sprinkled with silver and gold glitter and splashed with an assortment of finger-paints in a rainbow of colors.

Teachers are made strong to withstand the wear and tear of children's handprints, sticky kisses, and hugs.

They come with an endless supply of sugar cookies, jellybeans, and bandages.

They wear bright colors and carry tote bags filled with books, ungraded papers, lunch, lesson plans, sneakers, and treats.

Teachers are given special skills for mending broken hearts, understanding hurts, seeing out of the back of their heads, and looking into children's souls.

Their hearts and minds are filled with the joy of reading, a thirst for knowledge, and a passion for teaching which they eagerly share with anyone willing to listen.

Teachers are given the special gift of touching lives which is generously used to inspire young people to be the best that they can be.

Tee Carr

I Have Come to a Frightening Conclusion . . .

I have come to a frightening conclusion. I am the decisive element in the classroom. It is my personal approach that creates the climate. It is my daily mood that makes the weather. As a teacher, I possess tremendous power to make a child's life miserable or joyous. I can be a tool of torture or an instrument of inspiration. I can humiliate or humor, hurt or heal. In all situations it is my response that decides whether a crisis will be escalated or de-escalated, and a child humanized or de-humanized.

Haim Ginott

In Praise of a Teacher

For Mr. Porter

One of our best teachers is retiring, Lord, and we've all been asked to offer a brief tribute. I want to say something glowing, something worthy of him, and the statement that comes to mind is this: He showed up.

That doesn't sound like much, I know. But I am reminded of a little girl I once knew who came home discouraged from her first day at kindergarten. When her mother asked her what she had learned that day, she sighed and said, "Not much. I have to go back tomorrow."

How often we say that children grow up so fast, but that's not true. Growing up is a long, slow process, and kids need people who will show up for them, to teach and nurture them—tomorrow after tomorrow after tomorrow.

Not everyone is willing or able to do that—to put so much into a job that offers so little in the way of money or perks or prestige. So why did he do it? For over forty years? Because he had this crazy, unshakable idea that kids are more important than anything else in the world. So he was a teacher, and he showed up.

Elspeth Campbell Murphy

The Seed

The small one in the front row
The tall one you can see
The one who follows behind you
The little one at your knee

The one who got an extra hug
The one who makes you smile
The one with twinkles in her eyes
Who goes the extra mile

The one you thought about last night
The one who you took home
The one who likes to hold on tight
The one who likes to roam

Each one of these is different
Each one of these you know
And you will be beside them
No matter where they go

For in each heart and mind
You've sown a special seed
A seed that says, "I love you"
And fills a certain need

So remember just how special
And how important that you are
For it's *you* that they take with them
As they travel near and far

Angie Martin

How to Be a Good Teacher

(30 Ways to Enrich Your Professional Life)

Smile
Live each day with enthusiasm
Delight in the simple joys of life
Expect the best of others
Breathe deeply
Keep your life in balance
Know your subject
Stretch yourself and those around you
Read aloud daily to your students
Use common sense
Learn some silly "Knock Knock" jokes
Laugh heartily
Listen to the wisdom of little ones
Give your love freely
Practice classroom magic
Teach by example
Play daily
Sing
Celebrate others' accomplishments
Give a gold star each day to someone
Teach with a passion
Never give up on anyone
Keep the artist within you alive
Have faith
Always look up
Carry an umbrella
Play nice with others
Remember to say "I'm sorry"
Share your apple and cookie
Keep on learning

Tee Carr

Excerpt from
Don't Forget to Call Your Mama

Mama had that thing some teachers develop, the idea that her students were her children, too. Often when I visited her in the hospital, a nurse would come into her room and introduce herself to me and say, "Your Mama taught me in the first grade."

I must admit that I did have an educational advantage because my mother was a teacher, especially when it came to grammar. My mother was on constant grammar patrol at home.

Ain't was forbidden. So were double negatives. Put the two together and it was hell to pay, as in, "I ain't got no more homework to do."

"You *have* no more homework to do," Mama would correct me.

"That's what I said," I once replied.

Mama made me go out in the yard and pull weeds out of her flowers.

Words like *his'n* (his) and *her'n* (hers) I picked up at school. Also *are* (over *are*, instead of *there*), *cher* (here), *rat* (as in *rat cher*), not to mention the usage of a personal pronoun when it wasn't needed, as in "Mama, *she* went to town last night."

Those were all forbidden to me. So was, "Mama, where's the milk 'at.'"

Her response was, "Behind the 'at.'"

"What do you mean, Mama?" I'd ask.

"Never end a sentence with a preposition," she would explain. "It's simply, 'Where is the milk?'"

I thought I had it.

"Tell me again the rule on prepositions," Mama said.

"Never use a preposition to end a sentence with," I replied.

Back to the weeds.

I have no idea how many first-graders Mama taught during her career. Over the years, however, I've received a great many letters that began, "Your mother, Miss Christine, taught me in the first grade. . . ."

A nurse who was with Mama when she was pronounced dead at the hospital had been a student of hers.

I've often thought about first grade teachers. Most of us don't have the patience to teach children that young. Mama often said she spent the first six weeks of each year teaching half her class to ask permission to go to the bathroom instead of wetting their pants.

First grade teachers, I've come to believe, may be the most important teacher a person will have in his or her educational experience.

Reading and writing are the basis of all learning. First grade teachers teach that. Imagine being able to take a six-year-old mind and teach it to write words and sentences and give it the precious ability to read.

As for me, Mama taught me that an education was necessary for a fuller life. She taught me an appreciation of the language. She taught a love of words, of how they should be used and how they can fill a creative soul with a passion and lead it to a life's work.

I'm proud of my Mama, my teacher. On her tombstone we put "Miss Christine."

Lewis Grizzard

I Love You, Miss Patten

Latin was never one of my best subjects. Miss Bonnie Willbanks did her best to get me started in the ninth grade at Brainerd Junior High School. On her 100th birthday, I was privileged to visit her and offer my best wishes. She remembered me in all the best ways—but mercifully chose to forget all of my Latin mistakes.

My second-year Latin teacher was Miss Lillian Patten of Chattanooga High School. She was a great and delightful teacher who also was generous with me about my lack of Latin aptitude.

Shortly before Miss Patten died, I heard she was in a local nursing home, and I planned to make a visit. Someone who knew her well tried to dissuade me, saying she was almost comatose and recognized no one. I decided to go, nevertheless.

When I entered her room, she appeared to be asleep, but a small noise suddenly woke her. Without hesitation, she said, "Lee Stratton Anderson," not only remembering me but recalling my middle name.

"*Ego tē amo*, Miss Patten," I proudly said.

She raised her head from her pillow and stared at me. "No, Mr. Anderson," she said, quickly correcting me: "*Ego amo tē!*"

Lee Anderson

Oprah on Teaching . . .

"If I was playing school, I wouldn't play unless I was the teacher."

"I felt it happen in the fourth grade. Something came over me. I turned in a book report early and it got such a good response, I thought, 'I'm gonna do that again.'"

"I wanted to be my fourth grade teacher for a long time. I wanted to be Mrs. Duncan. Fourth grade was the turning point in my life—I discovered long division!"

From *America Online*, October 3, 1995, when asked: *Oprah, you are a hero of some sorts to many people. Do you feel that this has a great impact on your life?*
"Not really. If I weren't doing this, I'd be teaching fourth grade. I'd be the same person I always wanted to be, the greatest fourth grade teacher and win the Teacher of the Year award. But I'll settle for twenty-three Emmys and the opportunity to speak to millions of people each day and, hopefully, teach some of them."

Asked who has been her greatest inspiration other than the Creator:
"You're right—Creator's number one. And a whole series of people would be number two—with Mrs. Duncan, my fourth grade teacher, leading the way."

Oprah Winfrey

Some of the best stories are told in song. In his tribute to "Miss Ferris," songwriter and musician John Hartford presents a touching testimony to his elementary teacher. Miss Ferris stirred John's passions to learn by capturing his attention with lessons about the river and her "great big collection of steam boat stuff." After John grew up, he went back to visit her one Christmas. He realized that although time had changed both of them, they still had their love of the Mississippi River in common. Listen to this story of a boy and his teacher.

Miss Ferris

Now I had a teacher when I went to school
She loved the River and she taught about it too
I was a pretty bad boy, but she called my bluff
With her great big collection of steamboat stuff, Oh Yeah

She had log books and bells, and things like that
And she knew the old captains and where they were at
She rode the Alabama and the Gordon C. Greene
As the Cape Girardeau she was later renamed, Uh Huh

But her very favorite as you all know
Was the Golden Eagle, Captain Buck's old boat
This old sternwheeler sank and went to heaven
When I was in the fourth grade in 1947

Well, fashionable St. Louis society
Taking a trip on the Mississippi
Asleep in their bunks with an after dinner drink
They didn't think that the boat would sink, Oh No

Well, I know Captain Buck was a very sad man
When that old wood hull went into the sand
And Miss Ferris, she was sad for sure
But immediately her mind went to work, Oh Yeah

Well, she did some politicking that was tricky and hard
And she got the pilot house for the schoolhouse yard
And so, instead of studying, I became a dreamer
Dreaming about boats on the Mississippi River

Well, the St. Louis levy was away downtown
It was the lowest, and the funkiest, and the furthest down
An elevated track and a cobblestone grade
You could go down there and get hit in the head, Uh Huh

But the river was life, it was changing all the time
It was a street, it was the sluice, it was the old main line
Started reading the waterways, journal and all
Following Captain Fred Way and C. W. Stoll, Uh Huh

I used to work real hard to get my schoolwork done
'Cause you couldn't fool Miss Ferris none
And if I went to sleep or I weren't supposed to talk
She was a dead shot with a little piece of chalk

Oh me, oh my, how the time does fly
Time and the river keep-a rollin' on by
Now I'm not a student and she's not a teacher
But we both still love the Mississippi River

I went to see her this Christmas last
And we took a little trip back through the past
On the easy rocker, we looked at pictures
And dreamed our dreams of the Mississippi River

Oh me, of my, how the time does fly
Time and the river keep-a rollin' on by
Now I'm not a student and she's not a teacher
But we both still love the Mississippi River

John Hartford

She Makes Learning Fun

My favorite teacher is Mrs. Woolum, my first grade teacher. Every year she hatches chicks. This year in my first grade classroom, we hatched ten chicks. She let us hold them and name them. We learned all about how to candle eggs to see if there were chicks in them or not.

Mrs. Woolum is very funny. She uses different voices when she teaches us. My favorite is her Leprechaun voice. She talked that way all day on St. Patrick's Day. She makes us laugh and she makes learning fun.

Elizabeth Grace Musico
Elementary School Student

Back to School

When my husband, our children, and I moved to Tennessee, I had no idea how my life was going to take an incredibly new direction. As the children, one by one, entered school, I thought it was time for me to sit back and listen to the quiet. But the chain of events turned out differently.

The principal of my children's elementary school, desperate for a substitute teacher, walked into my son's classroom and asked if anyone's mother could teach. With all the innocence of a fourth-grader who thinks his mother can do anything, he raised his hand and said, "Call my mom. She knows how to teach." With one telephone call, I was no longer a stay-at-home mom. My teaching career began.

After only a few weeks with my students in the classroom, I knew that I had found my destiny. For 38 (and counting) years, I anticipated with excitement every day of school.

Each fall when the new students arrived, I looked at their bright faces and felt gratified to have had the chance to pass on my love and enthusiasm for learning.

Each student brought a new opportunity to my classroom. Every student represented a challenge that invigorated me daily.

To anyone entering the teaching profession today, I would pass on a bit of wisdom. Let the students know you care about them and their learning. The rewards of teaching come from within so enjoy each student and the possibilities that come with each new day.

And to that little boy of many years ago, my son, who loved me enough to raise his hand in class, I'd like to give him a special thanks.

Dorothy R. Leader

An Awesome Responsibility

As a staff development instructor for twenty-three years, I presented hundreds of workshops to teachers and school administrators. The participants ranged from kindergarten to community college levels.

One technique I used, a "quick think" activity, never ceased to amaze and inspire. The participants were asked to list, as quickly as they could, five people who had the most positive influence on their lives. These were to be people who were responsible for helping them reach their goals in life.

After three or four minutes, I would ask for a show of hands to find out how many had included at least one teacher. The results were always the same, whether the group included twenty-five or one hundred individuals. Invariably, at least ninety percent of the audience had listed a teacher.

As the participants raised their hands, they would glance around the group at the other raised hands. A soft murmur accompanied this glance, and the feeling of amazement was palpable. The impact was strong, the message was clear, and any discussion was superfluous. Teachers do indeed have a tremendous, lasting influence on their students' lives.

A teacher's responsibility is awesome and humbling.

Ann Tolstoy

Smell Good and Laugh a Lot!

Most teachers and principals want their students to remember them as individuals who were good teachers, who cared about kids, and who treated all equally and with fairness

In reality, however, it is the small everyday things—often unrelated to teaching Algebra, diagramming a sentence, or conjugating a verb—for which students remember us.

As a teacher, I wanted to be the best I could be. I always fully prepared my lessons, made them interesting and motivating, and treated my students with respect and courtesy. Later, when I became a principal, I tried to lead by example, create a family atmosphere, emphasize character education and good citizenship, and hold high expectations for all.

When I was beginning my second year as principal of a small inner-city school, one of my teachers said, "The kids really love you, Tee."

"Oh, really?" I said, happy to hear this compliment but wondering what I had done to deserve it. "Was it the field trip I chaperoned? I know they really had a lot of fun at the aquarium!"

"No, it wasn't that," the teacher responded, shaking her head.

"Well," I said, "It was probably the 'Back to School' party we had last week. They really enjoyed the games and refreshments. That was it, right?"

"Well, Tee, I know they liked both of those, but I don't think it was anything specific that you did. My kids just told me that they really care about you. You're pretty special to them." Then she grinned and said, "Several of them commented that you always smell good and laugh a lot!"

Teachers are loved for many reasons. Often it is the little things that children find so memorable. It might be the smile we give children, the pat on the back, the word of encouragement when they are down, the extra help with a difficult assignment, the hearty laugh at a silly joke, or even the scent of perfume.

After school that day, I went home and did a little rearranging in my bathroom. I moved my bottle of *Estée Lauder* from the top shelf of my linen closet to the center of my makeup table. I wanted to make sure I never left for school without dabbing on a little each morning.

Tee Carr

An Award for Mrs. Phillips

Let me tell you about my favorite teacher and how she became it.

It all started the day I tried to find out who would be my third grade teacher. I had heard that the best teacher was Mrs. Jones, so naturally I wanted her. When I got to school I found that I didn't get the teacher I had hoped for. Instead, I got Mrs. Phillips.

I told Mrs. Phillips I didn't want her as a teacher. But she said, "Dear, we don't always get what we want." Although I didn't realize it at the time, this was one important lesson Mrs. Phillips taught me. Sometimes what we think we want and what we really need are completely different.

Throughout the year, Mrs. Phillips made classwork fun. I remember learning my multiplication tables and our class challenging the fifth-graders to a contest. We won! Imagine that! Third-graders outdoing the fifth-graders! Mrs. Phillips was so proud of us.

We studied about many things, but my favorite was about Hawaii. We did the neatest things like learning how to hula. We had a luau at the end of the year and everyone in our class brought a special Hawaiian food. Many of us wore grass skirts. Our parents were invited, and we performed a hula dance for them. Mrs. Phillips danced too.

Learning is pretty neat when you are having fun. I wish I could give Mrs. Phillips an award for being my favorite teacher in elementary school. I guess this story is her reward. Thanks, Mrs. Phillips, for being a GREAT TEACHER!

Ann Marie Furr
Elementary School Student

A Good Start

When I was in the sixth grade at Glenwood Elementary School, my teacher, Miss Ruth Posey (later Mrs. Akers), allowed me to start a school paper, the *Blue and Gold.* It was produced, barely, in that light purple print of the old Ditto machine system, predecessor of Mimeograph and a far cry from modern desktop publishing, which spoils us all.

That was my "beginning" in "the newspaper business" which I entered formally as a 16-year-old reporter for the *Chattanooga News-Free Press* in 1942, while a junior at Chattanooga High School. Then in 1958, when I was named editor of the *Free Press*, "Miss Posey" wrote me a very nice letter and sent me a complete set of the *Blue and Gold* newspapers that she had saved for me all those years. I went to see her and had a delightful visit.

In 1990, when I became publisher of the *Free Press*, I received a wonderful congratulatory letter from her prompting me to pay her another visit to talk over old times. She was a great teacher who always kept up with her "children" over the years.

Lee Anderson

The Teacher Who Changed My Life

The teacher who changed my life was my second grade teacher, Mrs. Bishop. She was a good teacher who always challenged me and helped me do my best in school. Sometimes when I didn't understand something or when I was struggling with an assignment, she'd say, "It's coming along fine, Caitlin, but you need to fix so-and-so to get it perfect."

One time we were getting ready to take our standardized tests, and I was so nervous. She said, "You'll do fine if you just take a deep breath and relax." I tried it and it worked. I did very well on my tests.

I really liked my teacher and other people did too. When she left the school, it made everyone sad. All of my teachers had an influence on me, but my second grade teacher had the most.

Caitlin Schroeder
Elementary School Student

Celebrities Talk About Most Influential Teachers

When you think about it, somebody had to teach Einstein to add, someone demonstrated that first pirouette to Margot Fonteyn, and somebody introduced the blues to Elvis.

Those somebodies were teachers. And while many complain about the quality of education today, teachers have often made a massive difference in the lives of famous people.

In honor of National Teachers' Day, I asked several celebrities if there was any one teacher that made a difference in their lives.

Bill Paxton (*A Simple Life, Twister*) remembers during his senior year, "I was studying chemistry and wanted to be a marine biologist, but math and science kinda killed me so I transferred into drama class.

"I thought it would be easy and I could just skate through it. But I had one of the most inspirational teachers of my life, a woman named Rosemary Burton.

She's still living. She compelled you, on a personal level, to not show up to class unless you'd prepared your homework. She was one of these people you'd be so ashamed if you didn't do your best for her. I never forgot her."

Jim Carrey (*The Truman Show*) has had the impulse to be "on" ever since he was little and was a great nuisance to teachers.

"My report card always said, 'Jim finishes his work first then bothers the other students,'" he says. "I was good in school. I used to whip through it. I had one teacher who had a meeting with me and said, 'Look, I'll give you 15 minutes at the end of the day to do a routine.' And that's exactly what she did."

Michelle Pfeiffer remembers such a mentor. "I had one teacher who made one comment, and it was ONE comment and I think it changed the course of my life. It was drama class, and I took it to get out of an English credit.

"I had no interest in acting really and fell in love with the class and the people in class. And one day—she doesn't remember saying this—she said, 'I think you have some talent.' That was it. And I never forgot. And I think kids go through life being unnoticed and not really being paid much attention to and I think those kinds of comments really affect them. Her name is Mrs. Cooney."

Richard Dreyfuss (*Mr. Holland's Opus*) credits

Rose Jane Landau as "one of the most influential people of my life. Yesterday I learned what it was that made her a great teacher. I figured out it was the fact that she really believed that we were as great as we thought we were. And because she believed that, we were like kites. We were so relaxed and creative and crazy and it was because of her enthusiastic belief. I've had other teachers who were great because they were the exact opposite. They wouldn't give me the time of day, but forced me to work harder.

"I can still see her face the night we did 'Zoo Story.' She looked at me like I was God's gift. And because she felt that way, I was better."

Country singer-actor Dwight Yoakam started acting as a ninth-grader.

"I remember this teacher mentioning to me, saying he didn't know much about my family or parents' view of working as a performer, but he thought I probably possessed the talent necessary to earn a living as a performer in some way. I'm 43 years old and that moment still stands out in my mind."

Comedian-actor Damon Wayans (*In Living Color*) remembers, "I had one teacher in the seventh grade who was the only one to encourage me. I got a 55, failed everything. He's the only one to pass me. He said, 'I'm gonna pass you because you're a joy to have in class and I think if you can stay out of trouble, you'll be something great.'"

Sharon Stone's drama teacher, Roy London, left her a lasting legacy, she says.

"When he passed away, it was just crushing and devastating to me because he was one of my closest friends. I was lost and didn't know what to do. A friend brought over interviews no one had seen. He talked about how much more interesting it was to watch an actor try something on screen and fail than to watch someone have it sewed together in their trailer and come out and be fabulous. And I wondered if I would have the guts to do that. And I've been doing that ever since."

Actor-comedian Robert Townsend (*Hollywood Shuffle*) says a teacher not only motivated him, but taught him to be color-blind.

"It was a white man, Mr. James Reed. I was raised on welfare. My mom raised four kids, my dad wasn't around. And in the fifth grade Mr. Reed said, 'Robert Townsend, you have something,' and entered me in a speech festival. He'd have to come and get me in the inner city, gangs on every street corner, and he wasn't getting paid. I couldn't (ever) be angry because the first person to believe in me was a white man."

Writer Dean Koontz (*Intensity*) has become one of the best selling writers in the nation because of a teacher.

"The reason I took English had to do with Winona Garbrick, a teacher, a former WAC. She was tough, this small woman, but just like a dynamo, wore athletic shoes to work. She terrified big football players.

"I had her for English three different years. In my senior year I applied to various colleges. And we were so poor I could only go where there was a very small tuition. I applied to a teachers' college.

"Miss Garbrick shouted. It was high noon. I was basically a shy kid and relatively quiet. She yelled, 'Koontz!' from the other end of this hall.

"Really, it was like a western movie, when she yelled at somebody, everyone got silent. She started walking down the hall toward me and she put her finger between my eyes and kept tapping me on the bridge of the nose.

"She said, 'I hear you've been admitted to Shippensburg.' I said, 'Yes.'

"'And I hear you're going to major in history.'

"'Yes.'

"'And I know why. Because you're a lazy boy and history is easy for you and you know you can always get grades in history so you're going to take the easiest thing. What you SHOULD be doing is taking English because you have writing talent.' I was so impressed that anybody cared about me that much to make an issue of it, I switched my major."

Luaine Lee
©Scripps Howard News Service

My Favorite Teacher

My favorite teacher of all is Mrs. Hayes because she loves to teach and really, truly cares about my classmates and me. She is unique and wise and says she likes it when we catch her mistakes. Sometimes she is strict, but even then, she is very nice. Mrs. Hayes is 59 years old and is very healthy because she waterskiis and bikes. She loves to do crafts with us at school. She is the best role model in my life.

Mrs. Hayes gives out class rewards for good behavior by using her marble jar. When we are good, she takes a handful of marbles and puts them in the jar. When the jar is full, she gives us a treat such as free ice cream. Another way she rewards us is when we "go to the head of the class" on the special bulletin board that holds our pictures. The board has a star placed at the bottom. Every time we do something good, she moves the star up. When the star reaches the top, we get a surprise.

Mrs. Hayes is a teacher, but often she reminds me of an angel. She always treats us fairly and with respect. In my heart, she *is* an angel.

Natalie Smith
Elementary School Student

A Creative Teacher

Mr. David Camp was my fourth grade teacher at Battlefield Elementary School in Ft. Oglethorpe, Georgia. He was my favorite teacher because he was so creative and would decorate our classroom according to the subject he was teaching.

When we were studying oceans, he would let us make waves, hang streamers, and decorate with ocean animals. The room suddenly became an ocean! I made a poster of the ocean with my dad and grandmother on the living room floor at Grandma's house. I stretched a net across the poster board, pretending it was an ocean, and placed different ocean animals in it. Then I wrote an article describing the ocean. We even used the computer to look up the different kinds of fish and animals found in the ocean.

When we were studying about tropical rainforests, our classroom became a jungle with sound effects and pictures of snakes, monkeys, birds, and mammals. Mr. Camp played music that sounded like jungle noises and animals, and he even let us bring in real animals. What fun when our room began to look like a real rainforest!

One of our lessons was about the Depression. To make us more aware of how it felt to live during that time, Mr. Camp had us use layers of newspapers as "Hoover blankets." This allowed us to "experience" the desperate living conditions during the Depression.

In English, we had an exciting project. When we were studying pronouns, Mr. Camp let us bring our own CDs. He played our favorite songs and we picked out the pronouns. When we were studying nouns, Mr. Camp asked us to write as many nouns as possible on a roll of toilet paper. Nouns, nouns, and more nouns! After we rolled the toilet paper back up, we all got to take our roll of paper and wrap Mr. Camp like a mummy. He was our "noun mummy!"

Sometimes Mr. Camp played classical music in the room to make it a pleasant place to study and learn. In math, we learned dance steps to remember the "steps" in solving math problems.

Mr. Camp made things easier and more interesting to learn because of all the neat stuff he did. Thank you, Mr. Camp, for making learning enjoyable.

Meagan Nichole Floyd
Elementary School Student

My Kindergarten Teacher

I have had many good teachers, but my favorite teacher of all is Mrs. Linda Dyer, my kindergarten teacher at Harrison Elementary School. She smiled a lot, was always friendly, and had more energy than anyone. She always made me glad to come to school because every morning she would meet me at the door and say, "Hello, Stephen, how are you today?"

We did many fun things in her class. We took field trips to the Science Theater and to the Creative Discovery Museum. Once we even took sack lunches and went on a class picnic to a neat park in Collegedale.

One thing Mrs. Dyer did that I really liked was to let us have a mid-morning break and eat a snack that we brought from home. Sometimes Mrs. Dyer would surprise us by bringing what she called *healthy snacks*—like apples and raisins and grapes—to share with all her students. While we were eating, she would read a story to us. Then she would show us how we could act out the story by pretending to be certain people or animals in it. After we finished our snacks, the whole class would put on a play about the story. Sometimes we would laugh and laugh at how funny we looked.

We celebrated many things in Mrs. Dyer's class. When it was your birthday, she would give you a party hat and some candy, and everyone would sing "Happy Birthday" to you. One day Mrs. Dyer gave me a pencil and a bag of candy, and it wasn't even my birthday. She always made me feel special.

This year I am finishing the fourth grade. Even though I am not in her classroom anymore, Mrs. Dyer still waves to me in the hall each morning and says, "Hello Stephen, how are you today?"

Stephen Myers
Elementary School Student

About Mrs. Daniels

The teacher who had the most influence on me was my third grade teacher, Mrs. Daniels. She had this way of explaining things that made things seem so simple. She also let us become involved in our lessons and have fun at the same time.

Mrs. Daniels would be teaching us a lesson and she'd let us tell some stories about that subject. One day when we were studying about snakes in our science class, she let us tell about our experiences with snakes. Whether our stories were about rubber snakes or real snakes, it didn't make any difference! She enjoyed them all.

That year in Mrs. Daniels' class seemed to go by so fast, because we were having so much fun and learning so many new things. It went by too fast for me!

Katie Myers
Elementary School Student

Alarmed!

State regulations require schools to conduct two fire drills monthly. This particular month, I had forgotten the second drill until late in the afternoon of the last day of the month. I had previously scheduled a faculty meeting to be held immediately after school on this same day.

The fire drill was held at the last minute, but when the alarm sounded, two female teachers were in the faculty lounge bathroom. They both came tearing out of the lounge to lead their children out of the building for the drill.

As the teachers gathered in the library after school for the faculty meeting, I overheard one of these teachers say to the other: "I wish he wouldn't have a fire drill when I'm in the bathroom at the end of the day and getting ready for dismissal and a faculty meeting. He caused me to tear a big run in my new pantyhose!"

The other one replied, "Honey, that's nothing! When that blaring alarm sounded in the lounge, it scared me so much that I jumped completely out of my pantyhose!"

Darwin Lane

School Bells

Listen to the school bells ring.
Faces light up, hearts begin to sing.

Ready for their desks, their lessons, as well,
Pride and anticipation begin to swell.

Why do the children have such pride?
It's because of the special teachers inside.

Not only do they inspire and teach;
Young minds and hearts, they'll certainly reach.

This is why children love them so much;
Each mind and heart, they'll ultimately touch.

Curtis Adams

A Great Schoolhouse

Can you imagine a two-room schoolhouse? Can you imagine getting your drinking water from a well in a bucket, and all the students, along with the teacher and principal, drinking from one dipper? Can you imagine that many times students built the fire in the "potbellied" stove to heat the schoolhouse? Can you imagine two outdoor toilets, one for the boys and one for the girls? And can you imagine one teacher who taught primer (now known as kindergarten) through fourth grade and another who taught fifth through eighth grade, as well as serving as the principal?

Perhaps you cannot. However, beginning at age four (and I am currently a young sixty-five years of age), I attended my primary school years in a little two-room schoolhouse with that exact organizational structure.

In reality, it was one big room divided with folding doors into two areas with a cloakroom, now known as a coat closet. And, oh yes, we did have a small soup kitchen. Most of us, however, carried our lunch wrapped in a newspaper to school. My lunch usually consisted of ham and biscuits or sausage and biscuits. When we could afford to buy some soup, the cost was one cent per day during my first year of school, two cents per day during my second year of school, and five cents per day during my last year in the school.

At this schoolhouse, I had great teachers and a terrific principal, Mr. Bernard Powell. Because of my reading skills, I was double promoted from the first to the third grade. I remember reading twenty-three books during the first grade. However, I still had enough idle time to get that same number of paddlings at school and an equal number at home for getting those, plus many more!

Miss Martha Grisson, my teacher for the primer and first grades, was truly outstanding. She taught me to read with clear pronunciation, expression, and comprehension. Of course, I had no idea what she was doing at the time. She also taught me penmanship, and to her credit, many people even today compliment me on my handwriting. In addition, my teacher taught arithmetic and spelling, as well as how to respect others and their property. When I did not want to listen and learn as she wished, the principal, Mr. Powell, was always there to make sure I listened and learned the next time. He knew quite well how to apply the board of knowledge to the seat of learning!

Miss Catherine Denton, who taught third and fourth grade work, was just as interested in my education. She opened my eyes to the huge nation in which I was living and the even larger one I would have to cope with in future years. She continued, of course, to teach reading, writing, arithmetic, and spelling skills. Equally important, she instilled in me responsibility, kindness to others, and respect for my elders and their property.

Miss Denton also let me have my first cup of coffee. She once invited me to spend the night at her home which was located twenty-five miles from the school. The ride in her automobile was an education in itself for a young country lad who had never been more than four miles from home, and only then by walking. I woke up early the next morning to get dressed for school. When breakfast was ready, she asked, "What do you drink at breakfast time?" I replied, "Coffee!" I had never tasted it before. Coffee was for grown people, not children. So that day I learned to love coffee given to me from my teacher, and I still do.

In the fourth grade, I moved to a big city (by comparison) during the Christmas holidays. I found myself in a large brick schoolhouse with a teacher for each grade and a full-time supervising principal. This school had a cafeteria, a real playground, inside toilets, drinking fountains, and a furnace for heating the building.

Let me hasten to say that the education I received was not any better than what I experienced in that two-room schoolhouse with wonderful teachers and a great teaching principal. I can, because of this good education, read, write, spell, add, subtract, multiply, divide, act responsibly, and show respect for others and their property. That schoolhouse and those educators who gave me such a good foundation for future learning will never be forgotten.

L. Quentin Lane

Who I Am

It always irritates me when a speaker asks the rhetorical question, "Who are you?" You know you are supposed to come up with a philosophical answer, and, worse yet, you know your answer will probably not turn out to be what the speaker is looking for.

Except for a few times in church where I suspected the speaker wanted something like "I am a child of God," my answer was "I am a teacher." I had been a teacher for eighteen years.

When I became sick with a chronic illness, I struggled to continue to work. Five months into my illness, I admitted to myself and my principal that I could not handle full-time teaching, and I cut back to part-time work. That school year came to an exhausting end, and I tearfully told the principal that he would have to replace me. I had no guarantee that I would be well in three months or able to teach at all.

As the weeks went by, it seemed like a normal summer. However, when school reopened I felt an empty space in my life. My fellow teachers returned to work, while I sat at home alone with no purpose except to try to get well.

Oh, I consoled myself that I would never have to face the rat race again. I reviewed the difficult people whom I no longer had to tolerate. I remembered all the fifteen minute lunches eaten with a knot in my stomach, all the recess duties surrounded by buzzing yellow jackets every fall, and all the days spent separating fights brought on by spring fever.

I refused to remember my students' faces. I refused to remember their minds opening to new thoughts, eyes filled with the glory of solving an enigma. I started my new life of illness, and I did not look back.

The next year rolled around. I was somewhat better, but afraid to ever teach full-time again. I decided to do something else which would be less stressful.

That September the school system employed me to teach homebound students. They were incapacitated or sick like me. We could relate.

My first student was a senior who had just had a baby. She would be out of school for six weeks, and my job was to help her keep up with her lessons. I collected her daily assignments at the high school and drove over to her house.

Stacy and her baby, Tristan, had been up much of the night. She looked like I remembered feeling a few days after I brought my first baby home from the hospital. Her hair was straight, her eyes ringed with dark circles, and she wore no makeup.

Tristan, a darling round-faced baby boy, sat rocking in his infant seat beside us. He was her whole life now.

I wondered how my assignments of government and French lessons could compete with what was going on in her life now. We began our lessons with a list of vocabulary words. Inside of me was the old stirring of a teacher's heart. How could I reach this student? What was there of value to her in a vocabulary list? She wanted to think about her new child sitting there in front of us.

"Do you know what words are?" I asked Stacy. She was silent, glancing at Tristan to be sure he was happy. "Words are the building blocks of ideas," I continued. "Without words we cannot think but only feel. The more and varied words you know, the more you can think with imagination and infinite variety. Look at Tristan. What do you think he is thinking right now?"

"Well," Stacy said, "he is probably thinking about crying, because it is time for him to eat."

"Yes," I said, "now he can feel hunger, warmth, cold, and a tummy ache, but he can *only* feel. When you speak to him and he hears and associates words with meaning, he will begin to think. It is important to talk to your baby all the time, so he will learn."

We went on that day to learn several new words in English and some in French. We began to compare French culture and thinking to ours based on each country's vocabulary and phrasing of words.

Stacy was a bright young woman. In her eyes I could see the glow of new and exciting ideas emerging as we talked. When I said goodbye to her that day, she picked up her young son and began to talk to him, faces almost touching, hers forming a smile.

As I drove home, exhausted after that two hour session, tears began to flow from deep inside me. I sensed that I had just done what I was born to do. As much as the God-given color of my eyes is brown, my gift is to teach. That is who I am.

Paula M. Carnes

Observations of a Beginning Teacher

Always look, dress, and act professionally. You're a teacher now!

The teacher sets the tone for the classroom. Decide the environment you want and work from Day 1 to establish and maintain it.

Make your classroom a safe haven. Your students should feel safe and secure in your classroom, no matter how they might feel elsewhere.

The best way to teach is by example. Students learn more by what they see than what they hear. Always be a good role model for your students.

Be prepared to handle the problems you can, be strong enough to get help with those you can't, and be wise enough to know the difference.

If you don't know what to do in any situation, ask someone in charge. This takes a little bit of the pressure off and gives you a valuable learning experience.

Do what you expect your students to do: learn something new each day.

Being thoroughly prepared is the key to a successful classroom experience. In fact, be prepared for anything—it might just happen!

Be open to new ideas. Use these along with the ideas and strategies from others to develop your own teaching style.

Recognize early in your career the difference between being a buddy and being a teacher. Don't cross that line with your students.

Don't be afraid to say "no."   If your schedule does not permit you to take on new responsibilities, just say so. It is better to be honest about your available time than to become overloaded and frustrated.

Remember what a "Day Off" means. Leave your schoolwork behind and use this day to spend time with your loved ones. You'll return to work refreshed and renewed.

Remember that you're teaching more than ABCs or 123s. You're teaching life.

Shane Harwood

Students Speak Out!
Sound Advice for Teachers

If you want to find out what's going on in our classrooms today, ask the individuals who have a front-row seat—the students. For years I've asked students of all ages to tell me what they believe makes a good teacher. The comments I've received have been thoughtful, insightful, and right on target. Most students respect the teacher who makes them stretch to accomplish more, approaches tasks with a positive attitude, and treats students in a way that demonstrates that the teacher believes each student can and will succeed.

Research shows that nearly one-third of our new teachers leave the profession during the first five years. The reasons for this tragedy are varied. Some teachers initially do not make a successful transition into the school culture after completing their training. Others, after entering the profession, realize to their dismay that they do not possess the personal or professional skills required to be an effective teacher. Still others, who have the desire and academic skills necessary to make teaching their career, drop out when they become frustrated, stressed out, or unable to cope with the day-to-day responsibilities the profession demands. Too often these teachers became inundated with a multitude of non-academic problems or activities that infringed on the time they needed to focus on implementing classroom lessons and improving professional performance.

During my travels to schools conducting workshops and seminars this year, I asked students to think about improving the performance of teachers and the problem of dropouts in the profession. I believe these are interrelated because teachers who are happy with their careers and their achievements will likely remain in the profession, grow, and excel.

I posed this question to students: "If you could give teachers one piece of advice that would help them become *better* teachers, what would you say to them?" The following responses are from students ranging from first grade to college in classrooms from various states. Perhaps new and even experienced teachers should take a moment to listen as these students speak out.

∽

If I could give teachers one piece of advice that would help them become better teachers, I would give them these suggestions for . . .

Improving Relationships

Have lots of patience when working with children. Teachers need to be understanding, encouraging, and willing to help.

Heather Waldrop
Grade 12, South Carolina

Try to have fun with your class.

Elizabeth Grace Musico
Grade 1, New York

Remember what it was like to be a student and try to relate to young people and understand where they are coming from.

Amber Ghent
Grade 12, South Carolina

Teachers should allow themselves the chance to learn from their students. Learning can be a mutual experience.

Tara Smithson
Sophomore, University of North Carolina
Chapel Hill, North Carolina

Try to make each day different from the last. Don't get in a rut, but mix it up a little. And never let your students get down on themselves. Always make them feel that they are somebody.

Darrick Cureton
Grade 12, South Carolina

Holding Higher Expectations for Students

Expect us to do the best we can.

John Ingram
Grade 4, Florida

Challenge the kids more.

Caitlin Schroeder
Grade 4, Tennessee

Make us stretch to do better.

Tony Brown
Grade 6, Virginia

Never accept sloppy or half-hearted work from students. Expect all work to be the student's best.

Dana Anderson
Grade 7, Florida

Improving the Learning Environment

Smile! It does me a lot of good to walk in a classroom and see a teacher greeting students with a smile. It makes me feel good about going to that class.

Tai Hammond
Grade 12, South Carolina

Be approachable in the classroom. Teachers must be able to allow their students to come and speak to them without students feeling intimidated. Provide a comfortable learning environment.

Emily Cloninger
Grade 12, North Carolina

Vary your tone of voice. Using the same tone can be boring and ineffective.

Jamekia Ford
Grade 12, South Carolina

Be more supportive of students and remember that not all students learn the same way.

Alyson Blair
Grade 12, North Carolina

Improving Lessons and Class Activities

Be ready to try new things and consider new ways of seeing things. Have a sense of humor and adventure. Don't be so predictable. Change the ways you teach from time to time.

Charling Ja'Nette Carter
Grade 12, South Carolina

Remember that the class you teach is not the student's only class. A student may have just as much work or more from other teachers. Be reasonable with assignments.

Holly Smithson
Grade 12, North Carolina

Have more up-to-date teaching supplies.

Meagan Floyd
Grade 4, Georgia

Give students more choices in their classroom activities. Occasionally ask them what they would like to do.

Matt Fortson
Grade 12, South Carolina

Relate lessons to the student's everyday life in order to help the student understand.

Mic Carr
Grade 10, Georgia

General Suggestions for Improvement

Enjoy the time spent in the presence of your students.

Annie Goodwin
Grade 12, North Carolina

Never talk down to students. Speak to them with the same respect you would use if you were talking to an adult.

AdraAnna Griffin,
Grade 12, South Carolina

I would tell teachers to put their hearts into everything they do and love every minute of teaching. They must believe that they're making a difference and touching each child's life in a way that no one else can.

Deana Short
Grade 12, North Carolina

Give every student equal love and attention. Use teaching skills that involve all the techniques of learning. But the most important advice a teacher could ever receive is to make sure you teach from the heart every day.

Melissa Frisell
Grade 12, South Carolina

In reviewing these quotes from students, we see that good, solid, sound comments about improving teaching performance come "out of the mouths of babes." And yes, Melissa, that is the most important advice any teacher, whether new or experienced, could receive—*to teach every day from the heart.*

Tee Carr

Assignment: School Patrol

In 1994, WRCB-TV assigned me to cover the education beat. I immediately became the envy of my peers. They cover car crashes, rip-offs, crime, government, and politics. Not me! I cover the schools, although some would say there's plenty of politics in the schools!

In my "School Patrol" reports, I cover the leaky roofs, the fights, the weapons, the dress code protests, and the overcrowded classrooms and buses.

The majority of school stories, however, involve positive aspects of education. Sadly, many of these stories go relatively unnoticed.

I suppose that's human nature. Some weeks, nine out of ten school-related stories will be positive and uplifting. I often get no response or feedback about these stories, but the "negative" story is sure to strike a chord. It will be talked about, complained about, and waved in my face repeatedly as an example of "negative media." This occurs, despite the fact that some of our negative stories have often helped spur elected officials into noticing overcrowded classrooms, repairing leaky roofs, replacing old air conditioners, and hiring more teachers, bus drivers, and security officers.

Through it all, I'm grateful to have had the opportunity to visit more than one hundred schools each year, in good times and bad. I don't pretend to be an expert, but I feel that I'm a pretty good observer. It's my job to investigate, ask questions, watch, listen, and then report on what I've learned.

And I've learned a lot about the people I've observed. The following is a list of random observations from my years on "School Patrol." These are the things I've noticed:

- Teachers who get to school early and stay late.

- Principals who are constantly bragging on their faculty and staff, who honestly believe they have the best anywhere—from the rookies to the veterans.

- Spouses of teachers and principals, who paint, sweep, lift heavy boxes, and do anything else it takes to make the classroom an inviting place for children. I see parents of teachers do these chores as well. And yes, I see children of teachers, from tots to adults, pitching in. And none of these folks get a dime from the school board, county commission, or taxpayers.

- Teachers working second jobs just to make ends meet.

- Teachers coping with computers, printers, and scanners that don't always work; teachers who are frustrated when these expensive items often sit idle in unopened boxes, because no one can install them or the school's wiring is inadequate.

- Teachers going to school (as students) themselves, at night, on weekends, and during the summer.

- Teachers who take it upon themselves to set a good example for their students by teaching them the value of looking people in the eye, speaking clearly, giving a firm handshake, and writing a thank you note for kindnesses shown.

- Teachers who cheer for their school's football team, whether they understand or even like the sport. It's *their* team and they're going to show up on Friday night to show their support.

- Teachers who spend a great deal of time acting as surrogate parents, nurses, or psychologists.

- Art, music, and drama teachers who take children from the poorest homes who display no apparent interest in school and find that heretofore hidden talent, that individual magic, that allows them to shine as artists, singers, dancers, or actors.

- Vocational teachers who help students find their interests in life and turn them into welders, auto mechanics, carpenters, beauticians, or graphic artists.

- Teachers of the gifted and talented who constantly strive to find unique ways to challenge their students and make them aspire to be even better than they are.

- Teachers for the physically disabled, the angels among us, who perform miracles daily. From the tiniest preschoolers to brawny teenagers, these superhuman teachers tend to their every need. I see them nurturing, feeding, and lifting children upright while strapping them in and out of their leg braces.

- Coaches, club and cheerleader sponsors, band directors, and music teachers who are forced to spend much of their free time as fund raisers.

- Teachers who spend an entire workday dealing with textbooks, homework, and special assignments and then go home and spend an entire evening and most of the weekend helping their own children with textbooks, homework, and special assignments.

- Teachers who see that the children in their classroom get something special for their birthday or Christmas . . . because in some homes, there's no guarantee this will be done.

- Teachers conducting class on the stage of the auditorium, in storage rooms, on the bleachers, and in the cafeteria.

- Teachers requesting to be transferred to an inner city or rural school—because they know the students there need something extra.

- Teachers greeted warmly in the mall by someone who says, "Mrs. Smith, do you remember me from fifth grade?" More times than not, Mrs. Smith remembers. That always amazes me, because Mrs. Smith has had hundreds of fifth-graders. To them, she's the only fifth grade teacher they ever had.

- Teachers who spend weeks, usually in the summer, decorating their classroom with maps, posters, artwork, magazine covers, and all sorts of learning tools. And then I've seen them have to take it all down and start over when they're transferred to another room or another school.

- Teachers without a classroom who "wheel" their learning tools from room to room, down the halls, and up the steps.

- Teachers on the road going from school to school because there are insufficient funds to assign a full-time physical education teacher, music teacher, art teacher, librarian, or guidance counselor to each school.

- Teachers and principals who pull all sorts of incentives out of their hats (or out of their pocketbooks) just to get students fired up about learning—everything from pizza parties to pies in the face.

- Teachers at PTA meetings when there are far more "T's" in attendance than "P's."

- Teachers who buy their own supplies, because they gave up on any outside help years ago.

- Teachers who buy clothes and shoes for their students, who take them "Trick or Treating," or home for Thanksgiving dinner.

- High school teachers, who take it upon themselves to see that their students are ready to take college entrance exams, fill out job applications, buy insurance, and perform well in a job interview.

- Principals who insist that "good kids" be sent to the office from time to time for an *attaboy* or a pat on the back, because they want it known that every trip to the office is not a bad experience.

- Teachers who come to work even when they're ill because they know there won't be a substitute available that day, and they don't want to burden another teacher.

- Teachers and principals who work long past their retirement eligibility date . . . because they *love* what they do.

Every day I see something new that could be added to this list, and as time goes by, my list will grow.   I hope you're as excited about teaching as I am about my job. I get to "cover" the schools. And I love it.

I hope this helps to explain why I admire so many of the people I've met on the "School Patrol" beat. And I'm certainly not alone. Educators are admired more than they will ever know.

Many of us don't take the proper time to say it, but believe me, teachers and principals, you are being watched and appreciated. On behalf of the silent majority who don't call to complain about every little thing, allow me to say, *"Congratulations on succeeding in a most challenging and honorable profession. You get to teach!"*

David Carroll

We Accept Responsibility

We accept responsibility for children
Who like to be tickled,
Who stomp in puddles and ruin their new pants,
Who sneak popsicles before supper,
Who can never find their shoes.

And we accept responsibility for those
Who can't bound down the street
        in a new pair of sneakers,
Who are born in places
        we wouldn't be caught dead in,
Who never go to the circus,
Who live in an X-rated world.

We accept responsibility for children
Who hug us in a hurry and forget their lunch money,
Who cover themselves with Band-aids
        and sing off-key,
Who squeeze toothpaste all over the sink,
Who slurp their soup.

And we accept responsibility for those
Who never get dessert,
Who don't have any rooms to clean up,
Whose pictures aren't on anyone's dresser,
Whose monsters are real.

We accept responsibility for children
Who spend all their allowance before Tuesday,
Who throw tantrums at the grocery store
    and pick at their food,
Who squirm in church and scream in the phone,
Whose tears we sometimes laugh at
    and whose smiles can make us cry.

And we accept responsibility for those
Whose nightmares come in the daytime,
Who will eat anything,
Who have never seen a dentist
    and aren't spoiled by anybody,
Who go to bed hungry and cry themselves to sleep.

We accept responsibility for children
Who want to be carried and for those who must,
For those we never give up on,
For those who don't get a second chance
    and for those we smother,
For those who will grab at the hand of anyone
    kind enough to offer it.

Author Unknown

A Hundred Years from Now

A hundred years from now,
Nobody will remember
Who I was, what I did,
Or how much money I had,
But the world may be
A little different
And a little better
Because I was important
In the life of a child.

Author Unknown

Part IV

PARENTS

A wise man once said that there are only two lasting bequests parents can hope to give their children. One of these is roots; the other, wings.

Author Unknown

A Tribute to My Parents

Before I was five years old and in kindergarten, my parents said something to me over and over again. They even got my relatives to say it to me, as well as my neighbors and the local merchants.

Several times a day, I would hear, "Little Harry Wong, when you grow up, what kind of a doctor are you going to be?" This was accompanied by their pointing out to me, as positive role models, that my uncles were all doctors and that my cousins were studying to be doctors.

They told me that it was a foregone conclusion that I would be admitted to medical school, even though the competition was tough in those days. What they wanted to know was what I planned to specialize in.

Not being in kindergarten yet, I said, "I don't know."

And then came their reply: "You're going to be a brain surgeon, aren't you?" In other words, they believed that I had the intelligence to be the ultimate of all doctors, so brilliant that I could even operate on other people's brains.

My parents conveyed a message of high or positive expectations to me. For this I will be forever grateful to them, and I send them my love.

I exceeded their expectations. I became a scholar and a teacher.

Harry K. Wong

"If you treat an individual . . . as if he were what he ought to be and could be, he will become what he ought to be and could be."

Goethe

Graduation March
Not the Sweetest Song

What I'll miss most is the music, Beth. I won't miss the pulsating bass that rattles the windows of your car and announces you're entering our driveway two minutes before curfew. I won't miss the music that comes blaring from my car after you've borrowed it and reprogrammed all those radio buttons that took many years of playing with until I'd found all the oldies stations and National Public Radio.

The music I'll miss is the music of high school choir concerts, talent shows and impromptu piano recitals that took place only after we let you stop taking piano lessons. With you off in college, we won't hear Christmas music in our house in early October as you and your choir friends practice for the Christmas concert that has become such an important part of our holiday tradition. I'll miss the music that has sung the story of your first 18 years. As you march into the auditorium to the tune of *Pomp and Circumstance* and get ready to walk across the stage at your high school graduation, I want you to hear the music of your life.

Picture a young father 18 years ago. On those nights when you'd wake up crying from night terrors or another ear infection and Mom would nudge me out of bed and say it was my turn, I'd pick you up, and off we'd go to a far corner of the house where I'd turn on my music and we'd dance. You'd calm down as we'd twirl slowly to the same song every time—Bob Dylan's *Forever Young*. I'd whisper the refrain, "may you stay forever young," as I placed you back in the crib.

I remember the first live concert I took you to. Mom said she couldn't stand to go to another Peter, Paul and Mary concert and that I should take another woman. I did. You knew *If I Had a Hammer* and *Where Have All the Flowers Gone* before you ever heard of Raffi and *The Wheels on the Bus*. A few years later, while you were still in elementary school, Mom and I sat in a fancy hotel auditorium and you gave us a gift. The piano recital piece you chose was *Send in the Clowns*. I heard Judy Collins singing with you that night as you played so beautifully.

Of course, when adolescence hit, you found your own music. When you said you and your friends were off to a Cranberries concert, I joked that they'd have to sing very loudly to be heard in Texas from their bog in Massachusetts. I became my father as I listened to your rap music, told you to turn it down and wondered why they didn't write songs like *Abraham, Martin, and John* anymore. But then came high school and Mr. Boyter.

When I think about the music of your high school years, I think of choir and your director, Mr. Boyter. He picked up where we left off to give you a different kind of music. Your four years of choir built on the hymns of our church that you already knew as he taught you the music of other faiths and other cultures. I'll never forget watching you and the choir perform the African-American *Gospel Mass* in a beautiful theater in San Antonio. Seven standing ovations later, Mom and I knew we had been witness to a moment in your life you'd never forget.

Not long ago I watched you sing a solo to a packed auditorium at the choir talent show. Mr. Boyter gave you not only music, but confidence. If you are very lucky, you can count on one hand the people who truly make a difference in your life. You know Mr. Boyter is one of those people. Through personal example, he taught you about having a passion for what you do. He taught you about commitment and working with others and the joy of achieving a goal that takes sacrifice and dedication. Mr. Boyter has given you notes that will feed your soul in good times and in bad. You, too, are part of Mr. Boyter's opus.

And so, Beth, when the graduation speaker tells you the future is ahead of you and that's what counts,

I want to challenge that. I want you to look back into your past at the music that has helped make you who you are today. There will be new music waiting for you at Texas A&M. For now, on graduation day, I hope you hear a beat. I hope you hear the drumbeat of time. But I hope you don't walk in step. Find your own rhythm, you own harmony. May the notes Mom and I have given you become a recurring melody that wafts through the life symphony you are creating.

As for me, I'll miss the music, Beth. It's 3 a.m. right now. I'm heading downstairs. I need to hear *Forever Young* one more time.

Dick Abrahamsom

Dr. Abrahamson wrote this letter as a gift to his daughter, Beth, and presented it to her when she graduated from Klein Oak High School in 1996. Dennis Boyter is the choir director at Klein Oak.

The Twelve Days of School

Please sing to the tune of "The Twelve Days of Christmas."

On the first day of school, my children said to me, "Aren't you glad that our education's free?"

On the second day of school, my children said to me, "I need five notebooks, six fountain pens and an unabridged dictionary."

On the third day of school, my children said to me, "We need Crayolas, your old Victrola, one pencil box and a buck for a lock and a key."

On the fourth day of school, my children said to me, "I need a gym suit, tennies and shower cap, a sewing kit, some pinking shears, and five yards of string, one tailor chalk, two thimbles, one bias tape and something called emery."

On the fifth day of school, my children said to me, "We need insurance, don't forget our lunches and a deposit for our lab breakage fee."

On the sixth day of school, my children said to me, "You forgot my workbook, name tags on my soccer socks and the loan of your car till after three."

On the seventh day of school, my children said to me, "I need a camera, hockey stick and pink tights, a tuba in key, one chess set, one nose plug, one leotard, for my extracurricular activities."

On the eighth day of school, my children said to me, "Do we have some old shoes, food we will never use, books we're not reading, money we aren't needing, for some hard-pressed, needy family?"

On the ninth day of school, my children said to me, "I had my picture took. It'll cost you ten to look, for twenty you can buy the book; no stamps, no checks, just money."

On the tenth day of school, my children said to me, "Wanta join the PTA, the Boosters and the Blue and Gray, the band is selling key rings, and you know how you're always losing keys."

On the eleventh day of school, my children said to me, "Where is my cigar box? Did you pay my milk bill? I need fifty cents. We're going to plant a tree."

On the twelfth day of school, my children said to me, "Why are you crying, you're finished buying, aren't you glad that our education's free?"

Erma Bombeck

Excerpt from
CHILDHOOD on Schoolwork

The best that a parent can do today is to be semi-involved in the schoolwork of a child.

"Sign this test, Dad," said my youngest daughter one evening, her left hand casually draped across the top two inches of the front page.

"May I see the mark first?" I replied.

"It's not important. You and Mom always say it's learning, not marks, that counts."

"Right, and I'd like to learn about your mark."

"Trust me, I got one."

"I appreciate your sharing that with me. And now I'd like to see it."

"You mean you'll only sign for a high one? I thought you were an equal-opportunity father."

"Is it lower than a D?"

"Dad, you have to remember that a mark is merely the teacher's opinion."

"Is it lower than an F? Have you gotten the world's first G?"

"The thing is, she should have marked this test on a curve."

"I don't care if she should have marked it on a *ramp*. If you don't move your hand, I don't move mine."

Slowly, she lifted her hand to reveal a bright, red D.

"But this doesn't mean what you think," she said.

"Oh," I said, "it stands for delightful?"

"No, it's a *high* D."

"Good. You'll have no trouble getting into a barber college. Tell me, did you study for this test?"

"Oh, absolutely. I really did."

"Then how could you have gotten a D?"

"Because I studied the wrong things. But Dad, isn't it better to study the wrong things than not to study the right ones?"

And one of the wrong things to study is a child, for only a child can make you think that F is her teacher's initial.

Bill Cosby

No Help at Home

There are times when even the best teachers have to call a child's home and say to the student's parents, "I need help with a behavior problem with your child." My first grade teacher found herself in such a situation with me.

One Saturday morning Mrs. Eunice called my house. My father and I were the only ones present so Dad answered the telephone. Mrs. Eunice told Dad that she was my first grade teacher, and she was having a real problem with me.

She explained that I just wouldn't quit talking. She would call me down, but it did no good at all. When she asked the class a question, I would always raise my hand and blurt out an answer whether I knew the answer or not. After sharing all the details with my father, she concluded with this statement: "The problem is that Brent just talks *all* the time."

My dad replied, "I can believe that. His mom and grandmother have the same problem! It runs in the family! I don't know if there is anything you can do about it."

Needless to say, that was not the response my dear teacher wanted to hear. Receiving no help from Dad, Mrs. Eunice realized that she was on her own.

Over time and with loving patience and proper firmness, she finally convinced me that I needed to listen more and talk less. I have carried this valuable lesson with me throughout my life. Unfortunately, at the time of my problem, and from a family of experienced "talkers," my teacher found absolutely no help at home!

Brent Hall

A Team Effort

John (not his real name) had an excellent academic record in his elementary and junior high school years, and he continued this level of success during his early experiences at the senior high school where I was a guidance counselor.

After awhile, however, John began to experience some difficulties with his schoolwork. He was absent frequently, and even on the days John was in class, he was often lethargic and inattentive. The teachers noticed this and reported his problems to me.

The visiting teacher and I dropped by John's home to discuss our concerns with his parents. We emphasized that John had the academic ability to be successful in any of the better colleges and universities if he would only attend class and focus on his work more. We expressed our concerns for John's failing grades.

During this parent conference we discovered the source of the problem. John's father said he needed his son to help him deliver newspapers. The money from this endeavor constituted a large part of the family's income. In order to deliver the papers on schedule, John had to get up around three o'clock in the morning to begin his day. Since he was getting up so early, he would inevitably fall asleep in class later in the day. John's parents were unaware of this problem at school, since he never mentioned it to them.

This meeting helped John's parents realize that what they were asking their son to do was having an adverse affect on his education. These were caring parents who were eager to join with the school to help John. Consequently, they made sacrifices and adjustments in their home and work routines to enable John to get enough sleep and attend school regularly.

I continued to work with John at school and communicate regularly with his teachers and parents. It wasn't long before John's schoolwork and attendance improved greatly. I believe this story demonstrates the value of teachers, counselors, and parents communicating and working together to assist young people in their education.

John graduated with honors from both Lancaster Senior High School and from college. He then enrolled in medical school and became a doctor. John is presently a practicing psychiatrist in Atlanta, Georgia.

Gladys Robinson

A Day of Pride

When I was beginning the third grade, my family moved to Polk County, Tennessee, to the community of Benton. My parents enrolled my brother, Lewis, and me in the grammar school that was located on a hilltop overlooking the town. The school housed students in the first through the eighth grades. It was here that I met the 43 boys and girls in my grade who were to remain with me through high school.

I have fond memories of all my teachers, but I especially remember my sixth grade teacher, Miss Lucy Clemmer. The members of her family were well-known historians in Polk County. Miss Clemmer knew all about genealogy, and she tried to pass some of this knowledge on to us. When I was in the sixth grade, she made each student in her class a "Family Tree." She used this to teach us about the importance of family in our lives. Miss Clemmer was always doing something special for her students. When I graduated from the eighth grade, she surprised me with a lovely corsage of pink and white sweet peas for the occasion.

My brother, Lewis, and I were a year apart in age. However, in high school we somehow ended up in the same grade and were scheduled to graduate together.

In 1941, it was a real achievement to graduate from high school. Few people, at that time, went on to college, for graduation day usually marked the end of school and the beginning of work for most young people. Many graduates also planned June weddings and began their own families.

Education was very important in our family. Although Mama's formal education went only through the fourth grade, she was extremely smart and taught us to hold our teachers and our education in high esteem.   I know Mama lived to see Lewis and me graduate from high school.

The principal of Polk County realized the value of graduation to students and to their families.   He made a special effort to recognize the parents' role in their children's achievements.   It was his custom to present parents with "diplomas" when the last of their children completed high school.   On that hot June day in 1941, I'll never forget the look of pride in Mama's eyes as Lewis and I, along with both of our parents, proudly received our diplomas and "graduated" together.

Frances Forester

Your Own Grades

When your child is struggling in school, you have such a strong desire to help that you often find it easier just to do the work yourself than to use a middleman. A few weeks ago my daughter came to me and said, "Dad, I'm in a bind. I've got to do this paper right away."

"All right," I said, "what's your plan of work?"

"You type it for me."

Once again, I typed her paper; but when I had finished and looked at the work, I said, "I'm afraid there's just one problem."

"What's that?" she said.

"This is awful. As your secretary, I can't let you turn this in."

Needless to say, I rewrote it for her and I picked up a B minus. I would have had a B plus if I hadn't misspelled all those words.

And so, I've now done high school at least twice, probably closer to three times; and I've gone through college a couple of times, too. Sending your daughter to college is one thing, but going to college with her is a wonderful way for the two of you to grow closer together.

Although we try hard to inspire our kids to do good work on their own, the motivation for such work always has to come from inside them; and if the kids really don't want to study, don't want to achieve, then we must not feel guilty; we are not at fault. You can make your boy come home from school at three-thirty, but you can't go up to his room and stand there to make sure that he immerses himself in the three R's instead of rock and roll.

The problem is one that every parent knows well: no matter what you tell your child to do, he will always do the opposite. This is Cosby's First Law of Intergenerational Perversity. Maybe the way to get a child to do his schoolwork is to say, "I want you to forget about school and spend the next two weeks at the mall."

No, Cosby's Law would be suspended for that. He would *go* to the mall and he would take your Visa card, too.

And here's the whole challenge of being a parent. Even though your kids will consistently do the exact opposite of what you tell them to do, you have to keep loving them just as much. To any question about your response to a child's strange behavior, there is really just one answer: give them love. I make a lot of money and I've given a lot of it to charities, but I've given all of myself to my wife and the kids, and that's the best donation I'll ever make.

Bill Cosby

A Family Matter

A teacher, noticing how courteous and polite one of her pupils was, wished to praise her and teach the class a lesson. She asked, "Who taught you to be so polite?" The girl laughed and answered, "Really, no one. It just runs in our family."

Father Does Know Best

Each year the National PTA sponsors a "Cultural Art Reflections Program" contest, and this year's theme is "Anything is Possible." The contest has four categories: literature, visual arts, photography, and music.

Since my daughter Chara is in kindergarten, I wanted her to draw a picture for the visual arts category. Instead, Chara wrote a story. To be more exact, I wrote the story as Chara dictated it to me. Oh, I so wanted to "fix" the story—correct the grammar here, add some detail there—but that was against the rules, so I wrote it just as she told it to me.

It was a cute story that Chara called "The Little Cloud That Cried." My husband took one look at it and exclaimed, *"It's a winner!"* Then he dashed to the computer and e-mailed the story to anyone and everyone who had ever communicated with us in the last six months. While I agreed that the story was nice, I did not see it as an award-winning entry. Please don't misunderstand me. I think my daughter will be the next Dr. Seuss in years to come, but I thought she needed a little more experience in writing and would improve with time.

Nevertheless, I knew that Chara and all the rest of the students who submitted entries would receive recognition at the school's next PTA meeting, so we entered her story in the literature category along with an accompanying illustration she had drawn. After all, she told us she had just learned in kindergarten that every story has "a writer and a person who draws the pictures."

My skepticism of Chara's story did not diminish my husband's faith in it. He called all of our relatives and proudly read the story to them—word by word. He carried it to work with him to make sure everyone had the opportunity to hear it. He even showed it to his boss who was visiting from Knoxville. "Chara the writer" became the topic of all his conversations.

The night of the big PTA meeting arrived. There was an air of excitement as the ribbons were being awarded. I was working on my "it's not important to win, but to participate" speech to give Chara when I heard the announcement: "The first place winner in the literature category for grades K through 2 is CHARA WHITELEY." I gasped audibly. I was so surprised that my little girl—*my* baby—had won *first place*. Her first blue ribbon!

My husband was applauding wildly and smiling with his I-already-knew-she-would-win smile. He was immensely enjoying this moment of being the proud "father of the prestigious author." Then we heard Mrs. Barbeauld, the art teacher, make a statement that caused us both to realize that Chara had won not only first place, but also second and third. The teacher said, "Chara was the *only* literature entry in her age group."

This knowledge in no way lessened our excitement and pride in our daughter's achievement. She has always been a winner to us. Needless to say, my husband's conversations now begin with "Chara, our award-winning author . . ."

Cheryl Whiteley

12 Surefire Ways
to Connect with Kids

Be available.

Tackle a project together.

Smile and be approachable.

Encourage ideas and dreams.

Praise accomplishments, no matter how small.

Listen.

Let actions speak louder than words.

Include "let's" and "we" in your conversations.

Learn from each other.

Laugh.

Be a good example.

Enjoy your time together.

Note to kids who might read this:
    These suggestions also work for connecting with adults. Even moms, dads, grannies, and teachers want to feel valued, needed, and loved.

Tee Carr

Part V

DISCIPLINE

The secret of education is respecting the pupil.

Ralph Waldo Emerson
American Author

A Lesson in Humility

Schoolwork never was a big deal for me. I breezed through everything except math, and it seems that I was born knowing how to spell fairly well.

From the start I thought I was pretty smart but now as I look back, it may have been a gift from my parents. We always had a great variety of reading materials in our house.

Mother was a late-into-the-night reader, and Dad built her a bed with a large bookcase headboard. Her bookcase was always overloaded with books, often spilling over the side of the bed. While Mother always kept her house clean and orderly, her bed looked like someone had stood back and thrown books at it for a half-hour. It would embarrass her for me to say that, but I'll say it anyway since it is intended as a compliment.

Dad also had a bookcase headboard but his appetite for variety was less ravenous. In his headboard you'd find the basic books he liked, including Adam Clark's *Commentary on the Bible*. A German Bible always sat on his nightstand, and he read it more than anything.

So the academic prowess I possessed from the first grade, which seemed to come naturally through a lucky inheritance of genes, might have really been evolutionary or environmental. I was constantly pilfering books from their bookcases and salting them away under my bed—even some "restricted" ones like the works of Sigmund Freud.

Zeb was one of my good buddies who lived down the road from me. He was a year older than me, but I can't recall now if it was from starting school a year later or being held back a grade. He was not lacking in intelligence, but I remember being in his home one time and not seeing a single book or magazine. It amazed me.

He was the king of the schoolyard. By the sixth grade it was well-known that because of his excellent athletic skills, he could whip anyone. However, he didn't like schoolwork and usually sat next to me or another student who made good grades so he could copy off our papers.

School was a three-room building, and the principal was a gruff man in his late sixties or early seventies that we called "Fessor" Smith. In addition to serving as principal, he taught the combined fifth and sixth grades. From the day he arrived, we knew he was the boss.

Chairs in the crowded classroom were close together so it was easy to copy from another student's paper. Zeb took full advantage of this. I often wondered if Mr. Smith was ever curious about why Zeb and I had the same answers.

On the day of the big test, I concocted a plan to break Zeb from copying my test answers. I knew I ran the risk of getting a good schoolyard thrashing from him if he found out. My plan was to have two sheets of answers. I would place the sheet with the wrong answers where Zeb could read it. Between the two papers, I stacked my books so Zeb could not see what I was doing.

The test asked for the capital of Nebraska and I wrote "Gobbler's Peak" on the sheet Zeb was copying. It asked for the highest mountain in America, and I wrote "Billy Goat Hill." Some of the answers I wrote for Zeb were so funny I could hardly restrain my laughter as he copied away.

A few days later Mr. Smith returned all the test papers except mine and Zeb's. When we inquired about this, he said, "I'll see both of you after class." I began to get a little nervous, because we had discovered he was not an easy man to fool. Yet, I could not imagine how he could know I was responsible for Zeb's incorrect, hilarious answers.

As class ended, Mr. Smith told Zeb to remain in the room while he asked me to wait in the hall. I put my ear up to the door and listened as he told Zeb he knew that he was copying from the papers of other pupils. He said he would rather have an honest incorrect answer than a copied correct answer. Mr. Smith told Zeb he was smarter than he realized and would pass if he just gave it his best effort.

Zeb came out smiling confidently as I went in nervous as a rabbit around a shotgun. What Professor Smith said to me went almost word-for-word like this, and believe me, I remember it well:

"Dalton, you are a lucky young man. Your parents have a strong interest in your education and provide you with all the things you need to learn. But instead of being grateful and humble, you have turned into a first-class smart aleck.

"I have known that Zeb was copying off other students' papers," he continued, gathering steam. "I knew I would have to say something to him about it. Now I have done that. But young man, I want you to know I am much closer to giving you a good paddling than I have ever been with Zeb. In fact, you can count yourself lucky if I don't bust you good before you leave this building today.

"You embarrassed someone who hasn't had the advantages you've had in life. What he did does not compare to what you did. He was dishonest, but you were haughty and thoughtless about another human being. You intentionally humiliated him and . . ."

I could see that the longer he talked the angrier he became toward me, so it was a good time to start sniffling and offering to apologize to Zeb. Mr. Smith walked over to the window and just stared out while I was repenting to the chair where he had been sitting. He waited until I ran out of gas before he slowly walked back to his desk.

I just knew he was going to open the right top drawer where he kept that big paddle—an instrument of defense you could have felt safe with on a bear hunt. But he just sat down with a misty look in his eyes and asked, "Can you make this right with Zeb or do I need to keep you both after school tomorrow to help you work it out?"

"Oh, no, 'Fessor Smith, I promise I'll work it out."

It seemed he stood there for an hour while he thought. I realize now he was just letting me marinate in some well-deserved karma. Finally he said, "I'm going to trust you to apologize to Zeb for embarrassing him."

Knowing how I have always dreaded a good thrashing, I waited for just the right time to apologize to Zeb. He came over after dinner and wanted to pass the football. I apologized and he just said, "Aw, I don't blame you, Pepper. I had it coming. And it *was* funny. But don't you *ever* do that to me again."

I didn't, of course. Any day you talk yourself out of two thrashings is a good day. And you are welcome to copy that off my paper anytime.

Still, the best thing about that day was tasting some good humility pudding. It's good for you even when life force-feeds it to you. One way or another, it is coming, so keep your bib handy at all times.

Dalton Roberts

A Matter of Time

Joey Jackson, a middle-school youngster, had been responsible for a series of transgressions over the last few months that had escalated in frequency and degree. Although every attempt had been made to correct Joey's behavior, the problems became more and more serious.

The principal finally decided he had to expel the boy for the good of the school. He called Joey's mother, stated that her son's problems had severely increased, and scheduled an expulsion conference for the following morning.

Mrs. Jackson appeared at the school promptly at 9 A.M. and was shown into the principal's office. After taking a seat, she calmly stated:

"I've prayed about this situation involving my son, and I told God that I would place this in His hands. Last night God spoke to me and said that you should not expel Joey but should give him another chance."

The principal knew that Joey had been given many second and third chances by his teachers and counselor but to no avail.   His behavior had not improved.

"God talked to you last night, Mrs. Jackson?" asked the principal.

"Yes," she replied, emphatically, holding her chin high.

"Mrs. Jackson, may I inquire what time this conversation took place?" asked the principal.

"It was after you called me last night. I would say it occurred around 7:30."

"I see," responded the principal.   "Well, that certainly clears that up."

"What do you mean?" asked the mother, puzzled.

"Well, Mrs. Jackson, you see, God talked to me at 8:15 last night. He said He gave the problem considerable thought after talking to you and that I should definitely stand by my original decision to put Joey's little rear end out of school."

George Whedbee

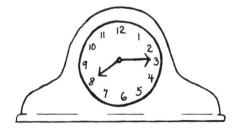

The Budding Young Lawyer

We always had strict rules at Anna B. Lacey Elementary School concerning student conduct, especially bathroom behavior. And, of course, in those days corporal punishment was not only accepted, but expected as one method of enforcing these rules.

One day a first grade teacher brought two boys to my office for causing a disruption in the boys' bathroom. She reported that they were swinging on the metal stalls and doing their best Tarzan imitation, including his famous yell.

As I quizzed the two culprits, I observed that the smallest boy was extremely frightened and upset, unable to speak as he fought back tears. The other boy, a tall red-headed first-grader, was calm and collected as he answered my questions without alibis or excuses.

Finally, the self-assured red-haired youngster said, "Mr. Gooden, if you will let us go without a spanking this time, I'll guarantee you that we will never—and I do mean *never*—do anything like this again!"

His appeal impressed me. "Boys," I declared, "ordinarily a paddling would be appropriate for what you did. But I'm going to let you go this time. Just make sure you stay out of trouble from now on."

As they walked out of my office and through the secretary's office, I overheard the red-headed boy tell his frightened friend, "See there! I told you if you would let me handle this, I would get us off the hook!"

Sammy Gooden

Ping-Pong in the Principal's Office

It was 1947, and I was in the second grade in Mrs. Cushman's room at Normal Park Elementary School in Chattanooga. Buses didn't take children to Normal Park in those days so either your parents took you or you walked.

Upper grade safety patrol officers, wearing special belts with straps over the shoulder and badges on the straps, stood on both sides of the street in front of the school. They carried red patrol flags on wooden broomstick handles and used these to alternately permit children to cross the street and signal cars to pass along it.

It rained one night, leaving mud puddles between the sidewalk and the street going down the hill from Normal Park. My friend, Martin, and I waited our turn to cross the street in front of the school and began walking down the hill. When we had almost reached the foot of the hill, Martin noticed a mud puddle next to the sidewalk and said, "Hey, Mike, watch this!"

He then pushed one or our classmates, Jay, who had been following along behind us, into the mud puddle. Martin laughed. I laughed. Jay didn't laugh.

Shortly after lunch the next day, the principal's voice came booming over the speaker box above the blackboard, instructing Martin to come to her office. I thought to myself, Jay must have told on Martin, and his mother must have called the principal. Martin is in bad trouble.

Martin was gone for ten or fifteen minutes. When he came back to the room, his eyes were red as if he had been crying. It serves him right, I thought. He shouldn't have pushed Jay into the mud puddle. I was pleased with myself for not having pushed Jay.

About the time I had completed commending myself for my exemplary behavior the day before, the principal's voice once again came through the speaker box: "Mike O'Brien, please come to the office!"

I walked down the lonely hall and entered the office. The secretary opened the door to the principal's office, and I saw the principal standing behind her desk with a Ping-Pong paddle in her hand. The thought ran through my mind that it was nice of her to invite me to her office to play Ping-Pong, but looking around the small office, I didn't see a table or any Ping-Pong balls. The principal came from around her desk, told me to hold on to the desk, and proceeded to give me a spanking.

Later that day, just as school was letting out, I protested my innocence to my teacher, Mrs. Cushman. "I didn't push Jay," I said emphatically. She gave me an all-knowing look and began quoting to me some words of wisdom from an ancient book: *Avoid the appearance of evil.*

I learned two things from that experience. I learned that if something looks bad, stay away from it because if you are present when a wrong is committed, you may get in trouble too. I also learned that my principal knew how to play a pretty good game of Ping-Pong without either Ping-Pong balls or a table.

Mike O'Brien

You Win Some

At one time in my career I volunteered to be a music teacher. I liked to sing, had a fair voice, and had always had some interest in music. I have never sung in a choir, however, and my experience with part singing or harmony was very limited. Also, I don't play an instrument. On the plus side, I can read music, though hardly well enough to call it sight-reading. At any rate, I thought that teaching music would be more compatible with my talents and interests than teaching five science classes, which I was doing at the time. So the music teacher and I, with the approval of the principal, simply traded.

He had become a music teacher in more or less the same way that I had become a science teacher. Our seventh grade teacher had transferred and a replacement was needed. The principal informed me that the other seventh grade teachers, who had more seniority than I did, were either unwilling or unable to take the job, so I had been chosen. Actually, it wasn't done quite that crudely. The principal we had then, a very nice lady, called me into the office and asked me how I would like to be the seventh grade science teacher. Since science was definitely not my best subject—when I was in college I couldn't even dissect my own frogs— I started to express doubts about my capabilities in this field, but she quickly reassured me. I certainly knew more than the students. And there was a teacher's guide. All I had to do was read the book, and I would do just fine. Nothing to worry about. I saw that I was going to be "persuaded" one way or the other, so I acquiesced.

I must say that with the aid of the textbook and a little outside reading I didn't do too badly. After a few years, some of the students even began referring to me as "Mr. Science." They were convinced that this was my greatest interest in life. I was aware of my own limitations, however, especially when I tried to help students who had a real interest in science which went beyond the limits of our textbook; so teaching music sounded like a sensible and intriguing alternative.

I had my own ideas about how to teach it. My main goals were to introduce some of my favorite songs to the children—classical, semi-classical, popular, folk songs—and to get the students to enjoy singing. I ignored most of the songs in our seventh grade music books (which led to a few less-than-friendly confrontations with the music supervisor), and brought some of my own records to class.

In the Army one learns a cardinal rule of survival: "Don't volunteer for anything." Nevertheless, I was sufficiently encouraged by my success in this new endeavor to volunteer for a music assembly. My classes and I had worked very hard, and finally, after many rehearsals, we were in the auditorium ready to go on stage. My homeroom class and I were the first to be seated. Then the others slowly began to file in. An eighth grade class had just settled itself in back of us when suddenly, directly behind me, I heard a voice call, "Hey, Greenstein."

The obvious discourtesy of not addressing me as "mister" left me with three choices: reprimanding the offender, condoning his breach of etiquette by responding, or pretending I didn't hear him. I chose the last. After a short pause, however, the voice repeated insistently, "Hey, Greenstein."

A few of my students were now turning around to look, so I decided, rather reluctantly, to answer. I turned and saw that the voice belonged to an eighth grader whom I knew slightly. I had noticed him in the hallway occasionally as he was talking and laughing boisterously with his friends. "Well, what is it?" I asked brusquely, trying to convey by my tone that I was aware of his discourtesy but didn't care to make a point of it.

Either the chill in my voice was not apparent to him, or he chose to ignore it. He grinned mischievously and said, "I hear you have a good voice."

His manner warned me that he was not trying to be complimentary. "That's nice," I replied shortly and turned away from him.

Evidently he was not ready to terminate the conversation. "Have you got a good voice?" he insisted.

"That's a matter of opinion," I responded. I hoped that the conversation was now at an end, but he was not to be denied his little game.

"I'll bet your voice isn't that good," he continued. "I'll bet I can sing better than you can."

Under other circumstances, I might very well have reacted like a "teacher," intoning a horrified, "How dare you talk to me like that!" and marching the insolent youngster to the principal's office. However, my class was scheduled to perform shortly and this was no time to create a disturbance. Besides, the boy had cleverly avoided using any words which were clearly disrespectful. If I had to explain the incident to the principal or to his parents, it might not sound like much. I would not be able to reconstruct his offensive attitude. He was probably aware of this and was counting on it to protect him.

I turned to him and, with complete self-control, replied coolly, "I have never claimed that I had a good voice. And since I have never heard you sing, I can't judge whose is better. Actually, I don't care. But I am sure of one thing."

"What's that?" he asked, still grinning.

"That my manners are much better than yours."

This did effectively put an end to the conversation. The assembly program was successful, I received some compliments from several teachers which I later duly communicated to my class, and the incident was almost forgotten. I briefly considered reporting the matter to the boy's teacher but decided against it. It wasn't important enough to "make a federal case."

The next day, as I was grading some papers during my "free" period, I was surprised to see the same boy at the door. "May I see you a minute, Mr. Greenstein?" he asked.

The tone of voice (and the "mister") was noticeably different from the one I had heard the previous day. Nevertheless, I was still a bit wary.

"Yes, come in," I replied. "What can I do for you?"

There was no smirk on his face now. His expression was serious and a little downcast. "I came to apologize," he said. "I had no business talking to you like that yesterday. It won't happen again."

I smiled, almost embarrassed at this turn of events. "You know," I responded, "there's an old song that says, 'What can I say after I've said I'm sorry?' I accept your apology. Forget it."

After that I saw the boy in the hallway occasionally and he invariably greeted me respectfully,

"Good morning, Mr. Greenstein," or "Hello, Mr. Greenstein."

Well, it's nice to win one now and then.

Jack Greenstein

The Assignment

Our fourth grade has focused on writing, writing, writing this year. Each week we have a topic ranging from those of a simply ridiculous nature to those which would require a quite serious response. This week we asked the children to draft a short paragraph about the best gift they ever received.

We began our session by brainstorming some ideas. The students called out examples of things they considered special gifts: mothers, fathers, their birth, Jesus, grandparents.

While the girls and boys were busily composing their rough drafts and completing their morning assignments, I noticed that Mitchell was "off task." This was not unusual. Mitchell's constant interruptions and endless questions were a distraction. He quite often seemed to require more direction and supervision than the others. After a few gentle reminders to "focus or else," the inevitable consequence occurred. Mitchell was given the opportunity to complete his classwork during recess.

That afternoon as we progressed through math, science, and social studies classes, Mitchell's behavior continued to hamper his learning as well as his neighbors'. Usually at the end of the day, I feel like Miss Viola Swamp of *Miss Nelson is Missing* fame— just an ugly grouch who hasn't made her classroom a loving place for its inhabitants. It was during this low-ebb, full of doubt, and self-deprecating moment ("What have these poor, precious children done to deserve a wretched teacher like me?") when Mitchell walked up to my desk to thrust his writing paragraph into my hands.

"Here's my assignment, Mrs. McCall. After you read it, you can keep it if you'd like."

I quickly scanned the third grade tablet paper to check for the proper topic sentence and any misspelled words. What I read instantly brought tears to my eyes.

> *My teacher is the best gift that I have ever received. She helps me learn my lessons. I love her, and I know she loves me.*

"Come here, Mitchell," I said as I put my arm around him. "What a nice thing to say. I can't believe that you wrote this about your mean, old teacher!"

He looked at me, smiled, and replied, "You ain't mean, Mrs. McCall. You're the nicest teacher in the whole world!"

Hindsight is always 20/20. I understand now how much Mitchell needed and wanted my attention. He was acting up in class to get it, even if it was the negative kind. To him, any attention was better than none at all. I vowed then to give him more of my time so he would not have to resort to misbehavior. How blessed we are with such dear, inestimable treasures with whom we have the privilege to experience life together for a year. Let us never overlook their fragility.

Laurie Massey McCall

Badge of Honor

My husband, Jack Carr, retired from the Chattanooga Public Schools after 37 years of service. During his career he was a teacher, coach, assistant principal, director of vocational education, assistant superintendent of curriculum and instruction, and an officer in numerous state and national education organizations.

Although he served in many roles, I believe the most enjoyable and satisfying time in his career was when he was principal of Kirkman Technical High School in Chattanooga from 1961 until 1967. During those years he worked closely with young men and women who were involved in the process of choosing their careers in life. The majority of these youngsters came from poor families. Yet, these same individuals today are the contractors, electricians, designers, plumbers, hairdressers, builders, and valued citizens who make up the backbone of the economic structure of Chattanooga.

As a result of Jack's position as principal, we are invited yearly as honored guests to reunions these high school classes hold. We look forward to these gatherings. Jack usually makes a short speech at each essentially saying how proud he is to have been associated with such fine people and to have been a brief part of their lives. These words, I know, come from his heart. He is proud that these individuals, once his boys and girls, have turned out to be hard working, church-going, family oriented citizens—loyal to their school and former teachers, and to their friends, family, and community.

Recently we were seated at the head table at one of these annual events. Jack was concluding his speech, and he asked if there were any questions or comments. One man in the center of the room stood up and said, "You may not remember me, Mr. Carr, but you paddled me when I was a sophomore." There was a hush over the room, for most people didn't know where this particular monologue was going.

The man continued, "I had been guilty of a serious infraction of the school rules and you told me I had to change my ways, that I was going down the wrong path and could get into serious problems. Then you gave me an option for my punishment: detention hall or two licks. I took the two licks."

The banquet hall remained quiet as all eyes were riveted on this man, then on Jack.

"So, Mr. Carr, I'd like to take this opportunity to thank you. You turned my life around. After that day, I got myself together. I finished high school and went on to college. Today I have a good job and a wonderful family." The man paused a minute and then asked, "Do any of the other fellows here have a similar story?" There was a lot of squirming in the room as people began to look around. Then, one by one, other men stood up, smiling at each other. One said, "Mr. Carr used the paddle on me too. I deserved it. He told me I was goofing off too much and not paying attention in class. I'll tell you, he made a believer out of me!"

An outpouring of testimonials followed. Applause and laughter broke out as this fraternity of men told their various stories, grinning from ear to ear, bonded together by their unique distinction: the proud holders of the *gluteus maximus* badge of honor.

Today corporal punishment in the schools is taboo. Most experts say it has no redeeming value, either short or long term. Today teachers and principals try to reason with children to improve their behavior or take away privileges as a punishment for misbehavior. However, decades ago, corporal punishment was accepted and even expected by many.

The situation was surreal. Here we were in a room with men who were proud to have been on the receiving end of a paddling. Maybe it's a guy thing, I thought. Maybe it goes like this:

"Hey Lester, we missed you at practice. Where were you?"

"Oh, I got called to The Office. Mr. Carr gave me two licks."

"Wow, did it hurt?" asked Bob.

"Sure it did, Bob, but it turned me around."

"How do you feel, Lester?"

"I feel great. It made a man out of me."

"Gosh, Lester, I really feel left out. I've never been called to The Office."

"Well, don't worry, Bob. Your day will come. Don't give up hope yet."

❦

After dinner, we were mingling with the alumni when a young man approached us.

"Mr. Carr, I didn't want to say anything in front of the group 'cause I'm kinda shy. If you remember, I too was having a problem in school. I'd been skipping school and you caught me one day. You told me how disappointed you were that I was wasting the best years of my life."

Jack listened to his story, nodding as he remembered the situation.

"You also told me that the only way to make something of myself was to get an education, but you said I was blowing it. You gave me the usual options for skipping school—detention hall or two licks. I took the licks 'cause I just wanted to get out of there fast.

Later, Mr. Carr, I started thinking that I didn't want you to be disappointed in me, that I wanted to make you proud of me.

He continued, "I didn't want to skip school. Most times I just didn't have any decent clothes or shoes to wear. But I didn't want anyone to know, not even you."

"If you had only told me, I . . ." Jack mumbled.

"I know, you would have made sure I had something to wear. I know that. I guess I was just too proud . . ." His voice trailed off.

There was a moment of silence as both men held their heads down in thought.

"So anyway, Mr. Carr, things began to change after that. I started coming to school every day. I got an afternoon job, part-time, that helped me buy some decent clothes. I guess I just had to do it on my own. And somehow things started getting better for me, and I began to feel good about myself. Anyway, I just wanted to tell you tonight that knowing you cared about me really saved me, and I appreciate it."

The man extended his hand to shake Jack's hand.

Jack reached over, pulled the young man to him and hugged him. I had to walk away.

There are many roads to salvation.

That night, as we drove home, both of us were quiet.

Tee Carr

Part VI

COMMUNICATION

All words are pegs to hang ideas on.
Henry Ward Beecher
American Clergyman and Editor

The Cross-eyed Bear
with the White Fleas

We often think we are communicating with children when, in reality, we are not. Although children hear the same words that we do, they may misinterpret them.

Examples of this are endless. We remember the child who recited "Mary had a little lamb, its *fleas* were white as snow." And we recall the child who began singing *The Star Spangled Banner* with "Hosea, can you see by the dawn's early light."

A first-grader from a parochial school came home and told her mother that she learned all about the "cross-eyed bear" in religion classes at school. Confused as to the significance of this lesson, her mother called the teacher for an explanation only to find out that she meant "the cross I'd bear."

The Lord's Prayer has taken its share of abuse from well-meaning children. One child began the prayer with "Our Father Who art in Heaven, Halloween be Thy name . . ." Another child, while reciting *The Lord's Prayer,* came up with a new way of dealing with financial problems through the creative use of amnesia. He prayed, "Give us this day our daily bread; And forget all our debts as we also will forget all our debtors." You will enjoy the following stories because they underscore the innocence of children and the uncomplicated and refreshing view they hold of their world.

Tee Carr

We Aim to Please

Young children want to please their teachers and are quite literal in their interpretation of perceived directions. Mrs. Lou Maynard taught a split first and second grade in a small rural school called Lone Oak Elementary in Sequatchie County, Tennessee.

Her first grade students were completing a science unit on animals of the sea, air, and land. Mrs. Maynard passed out a worksheet and gave her students directions, saying, "Be sure to put one line under the animals found in the sea, two lines under the animals in the air, and three lines under the animals found on the land."

The teacher began to work with her second-graders while the first grade group labored diligently on their assignment. When the first-graders were finished, she collected their work and looked at each paper to check its completion.

One paper caught her attention immediately because it had so many tiny drawings on it. As she looked closer, she could see that this little boy had carefully and meticulously drawn one *lion* under all the animals found in the sea, two *lions* under all the animals found in the water, and three *lions* under all the animals found on land. You can be sure that this precious child, who meticulously followed the directions as he perceived them, certainly pleased his teacher on this day.

Barbara L. Rigsby

School secretaries rarely, if ever, get a chance to eat lunch undisturbed. Usually they drink a cola and eat a sandwich while typing with one hand, directing a parent to the correct classroom with the other, and cradling a telephone on their shoulder. You'll enjoy the following story about a secretary who tried to schedule a few minutes for a lunch break.

Hello!

Carol Henry, school secretary, settled into the teachers' lounge to enjoy her lunch. She had arranged for a third-grader to answer the telephone for this short period and to come get her for any incoming calls. The lounge was only a few feet away from the office, and I was sitting across from Carol at the lunch table. On this particular day, the third-grader must have been delayed in reporting to "her job" because we could hear the phone ringing. I had a clear view of the door to the office, and I told Carol that I could see a student standing near the office door.

"Surely that child will answer the ringing phone," Mrs. Henry commented as she began to eat her lunch. As the phone continued to ring, she asked me if the child had gone into the office. I replied that he still remained just outside the door. Mrs. Henry put down her lunch and went to answer the phone.

As she came out the office door, she said to the young boy still standing in the hall, "If the phone rings again, would you just say hello?" The boy nodded okay, and Mrs. Henry returned to the lounge to resume her lunch.

Within minutes the phone again began ringing. Carol asked me if the little boy had gone to answer it. I told her that he was still outside the door.

Ring!

Ring!

Mrs. Henry jumped up and ran back to the office. When Carol returned, she was laughing so hard she could hardly relate what had happened. As she approached the youngster still standing in the hall, he was calling out "Hello" each time the phone rang.

Ring! "Hello."

Ring! "Hello."

He was doing exactly as he was directed.

Janet Ginsberg Perfetti

Don't Look At Me!

Communicating with young children is refreshing because they are so open to the world around them, and they perceive language so literally. In our adult world, we often fail to realize how children interpret what we are saying. As an early childhood educator, I mastered the art of speaking with one-syllable words, using simple sentences, and saying the same thing ten different ways.

On one particular occasion, five-year-old Kevin was telling me a "tall tale" embellished with his vivid imagination. I can't remember the story, but I remember saying to him at the conclusion, "Why Kevin, I think you are pulling my leg." He looked astonished, if not horrified, and responded, "Honest, Mrs. Hodges, I didn't touch you."

Eunice C. Hodges

To Go or Not to Go

Before accompanying her students on a class field trip to the theater, the teacher held a brief review to see if the students had a clear understanding of the play they were about to see.

"Let's see what you remember about the play we've been studying," she said. "Can anyone tell me who wrote this play?"

"I know! I know!" called out one boy with excitement. "Shakespeare wrote the play."

"That's right, Josh!" said the teacher. "Very good."

"Will he be there today?" Josh asked.

"No, honey," replied the teacher. "He's dead."

"Oh, great!" Josh said, rolling his eyes with disgust. "Does this mean we don't get to go now?"

Lauren Rickey

-

What Do You Expect?

My niece, Teri Lynn, was in the first grade at Crossroad's Elementary School in Marion County, Tennessee. Teri's teacher gave her students many learning opportunities and instilled in them the confidence to do what was assigned to them.

As on most days when Teri came home from school, her mother asked her what had happened at school that day. Teri said she had learned a poem in her class, and she began to recite it for her mother. Teri's mother praised her for the fine job she did and commented about how smart she was to memorize such a long poem. Teri brushed the praise aside and said, "That's not so much; you know I *am* in the 'exhilarated' reading group!"

Barbara L. Rigsby

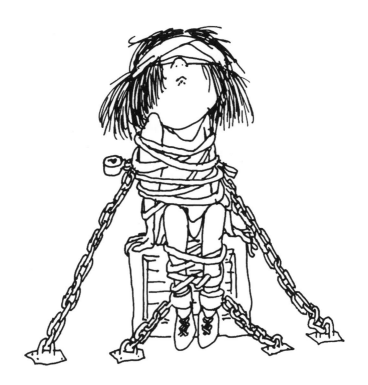

Kidnapped!

This morning I got kidnapped
By three masked men.
They stopped me on the sidewalk,
And offered me some candy,
And when I wouldn't take it
They grabbed me by the collar,
And pinned my arms behind me,
And shoved me in the backseat
Of this big black limousine and
Tied my hands behind my back
With sharp and rusty wire.
Then they put a blindfold on me
So I couldn't see where they took me,
And plugged up my ears with cotton
So I couldn't hear their voices.
And drove for 20 miles or
At least for 20 minutes, and then
Dragged me from the car down to
Some cold and moldy basement,
Where they stuck me in a corner
And went off to get the ransom
Leaving one of them to guard me
With a shotgun pointed at me,
Tied up sitting on a stool . . .
That's why I'm late for school!

Shel Silverstein

Let's Get This Right!

A kindergarten child enters the school office.

The secretary glances at the clock and asks the child, "Are you tardy, honey?"

"Oh, no, I not tardy," the student replies. "I just be late."

Watch Your Language!

One day in the lunch room, a little girl came to me and said, "Mrs. Memory, I think you need to talk to James. He's over there talking *cursive!*"

Catherine S. Memory

Dear Teacher

Teachers frequently receive notes from parents asking for information or requesting that their children be excused from class for one reason or another. Sometimes the notes are hurriedly written by parents when they are trying to get their brood ready for school, and in some cases, even while transporting their children to school. It is no surprise that many of these notes do not communicate exactly what the parent intended. We have included a few of the more interesting notes in this chapter for your enjoyment. (To relieve your mind, we have changed the names.)

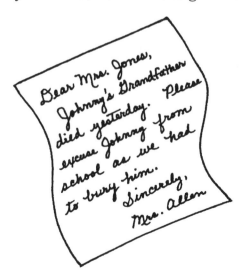

Dear Mrs. Jones,
Johnny's Grandfather died yesterday. Please excuse Johnny from school as we had to bury him.
Sincerely,
Mrs. Allen

Dear Mrs. Patten,
Jennifer could not come to school today because she is bothered by very close veins.
Thank you.
Mrs. Eberly

Dear Teacher,
Arnie won't be at school tomorrow. A mean dog bit him on the leg and the vet had to put him away.
Sincerely,
Joe Dover

Veterans All!

The first grade students had noticed the flags flying on Veterans Day.

One student asked, "What's a veteran?"

The second student replied, "Oh, that's a person who works on horses, dogs, cats, and stuff."

The third student said with confidence, "No, you're wrong! Everybody knows a veteran is a person who doesn't eat meat."

Lauren Rickey

Independence Day

The teacher noticed that one of her students was holding his side. She approached him to find out what the problem was.

"My side hurts," said the child.

"Really? From what?" asked the teacher, concerned.

"I think it's from where I had my independence took out."

Lauren Rickey

You Need What?

Stanley, a kindergartner, had brand new glasses but was too embarrassed to wear them to school. To make him feel better and encourage him to wear his glasses, the children and I told Stanley how good his glasses looked.

While we were admiring the glasses during Circle Time, another young boy in the group raised his hand and said, "Mrs. Horton, I think I need some condoms."

Somewhat shocked, but thinking I had not heard him correctly, I said, "Excuse me, *what* do you need?"

He replied innocently, "I can't see too good, Mrs. Horton. That's why I need to get some condoms. My mom has a pair and wears them instead of glasses."

After picking my jaw up off the floor, I realized what he meant.

Deborah Horton

Too Many Infomercials!

While studying dinosaurs, my kindergarten students used a View Master™ to look at pictures of the dinos. Later that same day while standing in line to go to lunch, I noticed that we were entertaining important visitors in the school. I was so proud of my students because they were well behaved and quiet.

Then Tamara came running down the hall shouting, "Mrs. Horton, Mrs. Horton, is it my turn to use the Thigh Master™ today?" You can imagine that I spent the next few minutes trying to explain to our surprised guests that in kindergarten View Master and Thigh Master meant the same thing.

Deborah Horton

Royalty

Several years ago, as a first-year principal, I replaced a gentleman who retired after thirty years at DuPont Elementary School. Darwin Lane was respected by families and students of the school and continues to be a valuable community leader.

Children of the community knew he would be their principal when they went to school. Misha, the youngest child of a family of four children, was beginning kindergarten. His three sisters had attended DuPont so Misha was expecting his principal to be Mr. Lane.

When I was introduced to Misha as the principal, he was very quiet. Later, he asked his mother, "If they have PRINCipals, why isn't she called the QUEENipal?"

Eunice C. Hodges

DEAR TEACHER,
PLEASE EXCUSE JANIE
FROM SCHOOL. SHE HAD
TO GO TO THE EMERGENCY
ROOM LAST NIGHT.
SHE HAD AN IMPACTED
VOWEL.
MRS. BAKER

Dear Teacher,
My son Howard
is under a doctor's
care and should not
take P. E. Please
execute him.
Mrs. Wagner

Dear Teacher,
    Please excuse Mary for being absent yesterday. She was sick and I had her shot.
        Mrs. Anderson

Dear Teacher,
    Please excuse Fred for being. It was his father's fault.
        Mrs. Jackson

Make Up Your Mind

Roy had repeated the first grade several times. One day we had a spelling test, and I noticed that Roy had pushed his desk close to another child's desk in the next aisle.

"Roy, move your desk back where it was," I said. "I want to see what *you* can do on this test."

"O.K., Mrs. Memory," he replied, "but I thought you wanted me to make an A!"

Catherine S. Memory

Oops!

My kindergarten class was making peanut butter cookies, and I was using the blender to mix the ingredients. The children gathered around me, watching closely as I added each item.

"In goes the flour," I said. "Next we add the milk and sugar. And now the peanut butter."

The children were responding with "Yum, Yum" and "I can't wait!"

I turned on the blender and one child called out, "Oh, Mrs. Horton, how neat! You've got a daiquiri-maker. Just like my mom!"

Deborah Horton

Dear Teacher,
    What's going on over
there at that school?
My boy Ralph says this
week is impotent cause
you're giving out testes.
Don't give him *nothing*
until you check with
me first!
        Fred Dutton

Eavesdropping in the Office

The school office is the hub of the school—a busy, sometimes hectic place—where teachers and students come and go while picking up classroom mail and memos, turning in lunch, field trip, or fund-raising money, and communicating any problems or concerns to the secretary or principal. Let's listen in on some comments from students made during the first few minutes of the school day.

Anybody seen my blue jacket?

My tummy hurts.

I left my lunch box and need to call my mama.

We missed the bus and had to walk.

Alonzo said I eat grass!

Where's my teacher? Is she in here?

I can't find my math homework.

He hit me, and I didn't do nothin' to him!

I can't find my blue jacket.

See if you can see a bump on my tongue.

Am I in the right place? This is my first day at this school.

Anyone found my lunch money?

I need a Band-Aid. My knee's bleeding.

Where's the mail for Mrs. Black?

We're late 'cause the bus was late.

I need a tardy slip.

Do we have a "lost and found?"

Mrs. Jones said to come quick! The boys' bathroom is overflowing.

Which way to the supply room?

Miss Smith found this lunch money on the floor of the cafeteria.

Do we have music today?

Joey said the F word.

My locker is stuck and I can't get my books.

I need another permission slip for the field trip 'cause I lost mine.

Teacher said I was fighting.

It's my birthday today.

I have a note for the principal from my mama.

The bus driver said me and Jeremy can't ride the bus no more.

Somebody lost their blue jacket and I found it.

Where's the custodian? Rosie threw up in the cafeteria.

Wanna buy a calendar?

I lost my breakfast ticket.

Is the field trip today?

How come I got sent to the office? We was *both* fighting.

Jeremy's popping pencils again!

I'm turning in some math homework somebody lost.

Can I borrow money for a pencil until tomorrow?

Our substitute teacher isn't here yet.

Margie is crying and we don't know why.

I'm sick!

I wanna go home!

The last statement was made by the school secretary!

Tee Carr

White Cows and
Little Green Men

Teachers periodically receive love notes from their students. They are delivered in the form of silly valentines, crayon drawings, construction paper creations, or simple pinecone Christmas ornaments.

Parents too receive their share of love notes. Moms and dads and grannies tape them on refrigerator doors, wear them proudly, or place them on mantels for all to see. Popsicle sticks, glue, and glitter are the mainstays of many of these presents.

Over the years my children presented me with many gifts that they made in school, Cub or Brownie Scouts. I still have them today. Two love notes my boys gave me hold honored places on the shelves in my living room—thirty years after I received them. One is a figure of a small white shiny cow created from a handful of clay in art class. The other is also a ceramic figure that resembles a short, fat green man—or possibly an elf—with a yellow flower on his head. I'm really not sure what it is supposed to be; this is my opinion only. No matter what the artistic interpretation, however, I wouldn't take anything for these masterpieces.

No teacher or parent needs words to interpret the meaning of items such as these. They tell us we are loved. These priceless treasures convey affection, tenderness, pride, devotion, humor, and the value of family ties. The communication is loud and clear.

Tee Carr

Part VII

PROBLEM SOLVING

The greater the obstacle, the more glory in overcoming it.

Jean Baptiste Moliére
French Actor and Playwright

Flub-ups and Flutterbys

The months prior to the opening of school are always busy ones for principals. In the fall of 1989, I had the task of converting a facility that previously housed an older junior high school into an elementary school that would serve kindergarten through fifth grade children.

As principal, I wanted to make the building colorful, appealing, and inviting to the incoming students. I heard about two parents, Sherry and Brenda, who had a small business painting murals depicting children and book characters for school classrooms and halls.

I contacted the parents to ask if they would paint a mural of young children for my school entrance hall. I gave them a description of what I wanted: smiling, excited children holding school books, pencils, and tablets. I thought the students at each end of the group should have their arms extended as if they were welcoming other children, parents, and members of the community to our school.

Sherry and Brenda were eager to begin the task. They set up ladders, scaffolding, and drop cloths and began to measure and mix their paints. Our front hall soon looked like a construction site.

Periodically I'd observe the artists as they painted, fascinated with the way they worked their magic to make the images of the children so lifelike. Every few hours I would find an excuse to walk by the painting to see how it was progressing.

A few days later, the artists applied their finishing touches to the mural. I watched as Sherry mixed paint to complete the pink blouse of one of the figures. As she stretched to paint a highlight on the ruffle of the child's collar, a glob of pink paint escaped her brush and splattered on the white background.

"Oh, no!" I murmured as I looked at the pink splotch on the wall. I watched Sherry's perplexed expression as she too noticed the accidental splatter of paint. She quietly studied the problem for a full minute.

I walked over to where Sherry was perched on the ladder, looked up at her, and commented as she continued to stare at the wall, "Perhaps it will come off without leaving a stain."

"No need to remove it," she said. Sherry grasped her brush a little tighter and began to work intently on the glob.

I moved closer and strained my neck to see what she was doing.

"There!" she said, smiling, as she turned to me and pointed proudly to her creation.

I had to smile too when I saw what she had done.

The child on the right of the group whose arm was extended in a welcoming pose now appeared to be reaching for something—and that *something* was a beautiful, delicate pink butterfly that just happened to be fluttering by!

I couldn't believe it. With some thought, a little creativity, and a few deliberate brush strokes, she had transformed a flub-up into a mark of beauty.

Over the years people have commented about our entrance hall mural, saying that the painting's focus on children states what our school is all about. Many parents tell us that the child stretching for the butterfly

254 School Bells and Inkwells

touches them in a special way. To many of them, it seems to symbolize young people reaching for their goals and dreams.

Life is not always neat and orderly. Sometimes it doesn't go as we plan. In fact, on occasion it gets a little messy and we make mistakes. Young people need to know that it's O.K. to make mistakes if they can learn from them, recover from them, and go on. Sometimes, with a little imagination and know-how, they might even turn a boo-boo into a butterfly.

Tee Carr

Class Meetings, Democracy, and Stop Signs

When Whit came in from recess, he must have gone right over to the bookshelf where we keep the folder for the agenda for our weekly class meetings. The last time I had glanced at it, there weren't any new problems or concerns written on it for us to discuss, so I figured we'd make a round of compliments and that would be all for today. We always start our class meeting that way—on a positive note—and then we discuss any problems and decide on solutions.

However, on checking the agenda again, we noticed that Whit had written that he was annoyed at the way students were passing him in line. There was a murmur of agreement that this was bothering several students in the class, so we began our class meeting with this problem as our topic. After some discussion, we found that the problem was occurring when the class was coming in from recess and the kids were jockeying for position to be first in line to get water.

We then discussed possible solutions to the problem. Several children voiced their opinions. Mayra suggested that after recess students shouldn't be allowed to go straight to the sink in the corner of the room to get water, but that they should go to their desks and wait to be called in some sort of turn-taking order.

It pleased me that we were closing in on a satisfying solution. Then Yumar spoke up and said, "We should just wear stop signs on our backs to tell the people behind us not to come around!" He got a round of chuckles.

I asked for final comments, reviewed the suggested solutions, told the children to cover their eyes, and vote for the solution they thought would work best. Yumar's "stop sign solution" was last on the list and received eleven votes which was half of the class. I was provoked at the giggles I heard as the majority of the class raised their hands for this, unaware of how many were going along with the joke. "Well," I said, with resignation, wondering about the merits of democracy, "I'll get you some red construction paper first thing tomorrow morning."

Some of the implications of the vote began to sink in the following day when I gave instructions on drawing an octagon. This turned out to be a formidable task for some. When printing the stop sign, I had to remind Robert that the "t" comes before the "o," not after it. I wondered once again how a boy whose memory of castles and moats and judges and courtrooms and so many other wonderful things is ironclad, but he cannot put letters in the correct order. Finally, when our task was completed, I asked the students to come to my desk so I could pin the signs on their backs.

"Do we have to wear them all day?" they asked.

"Yes, we are not going to put them on and take them off," I responded, trying to mask my irritation at their selection of a silly solution to a very real problem. Inwardly, however, I was pleased that they were finally realizing they had created the predicament they were in. Yes, they had voted and giggled at Yumar's goofiness, but now they were stuck with walking around the school with red stop signs pinned to their backs.

What would the other students say? We soon found out.

"What's that sign for?" "Why don't you put 'Kick Me!' on your sign?" These were only a few of the endless comments my students endured at lunchtime.

Emily wrote in her journal the next morning that all day she had tried to walk with her back to the wall.

The coveted duty of carrying the boxes of computer keyboards back to the storage area in the main building had only increased my students' misery, because they had to walk past the fifth-graders at lunchtime. What a cacophony of jeers and pointing fingers!

The next afternoon, the class requested a special "called meeting." Various students described their embarrassment at having to wear the stop signs and having to bear the ridicule of their peers. There was an outcry among the group to come up with some solution, *any* solution, which would move smoothly and quickly and would be based on something sensible like taking turns.

Another vote was immediately taken. A frustrated, badgered, maligned group of students held up their right hands for their favorite choice. Only Yumar voted to retain the stop sign solution. I was the only one who saw his upraised hand in the back of the room, and my lips are forever sealed.

Anne Knight Watson

Weed Awound

A colleague of mine related this story about a well-known reading specialist who was evaluating a young student's reading ability. As the specialist carefully listened to the first-grader read the selections aloud, he noticed that although she had some difficulty articulating her "r's," she read with great fluency and speed. He smiled as the little girl verbally danced over the words and phrases. When she encountered the more difficult words, she just ad-libbed and kept on going.

"My, my, you read very well," he stated as the little girl grinned from ear to ear, "but I noticed that you didn't try to figure out some of the harder words. You either skipped them or made up other words for them. Could you tell me why you did that?"

"Well," she said as she explained her method, "when I see some wowds that I don't know, I just weed awound 'em."

"Weed awound them?" the expert asked with a puzzled look on his face.

"Yes, I willy don't wowwy 'bout those wowds," she replied, smiling, "I just weed awound them and keep on going."

There is a life lesson here someplace. "Weeding Awound" seems like a good solution to many problems we encounter in life.

We know that we will occasionally hit a bump as we proceed down the highway of life. If we live long enough, we will face illness, despair, loss, and death. We must not let those potholes of tragedy cause us to screech our lives to a halt, to become immersed in our grief. We must find a detour, a way to bypass them, in order to keep moving forward. We must weed awound our difficulties the best way we can.

The story of Christopher Reeve, the movie actor, is a good example of this. When Reeve had the tragic accident on his horse in 1997, most people thought that because of his severe spinal cord injury, there was no way he could recover to have a life worth living. This was a man who could neither breathe without the aid of a machine nor move his body from the neck down. To our amazement, however, Reeve showed just how tough he was. He turned adversity into a challenge, became a role model for the physically disabled, and lived to inspire millions of people. Today he has resumed his career as an actor and movie director, and he is currently a spokesperson for numerous charities and organizations.

There are countless people from all walks of life who have mirrored Reeve's achievement. Every day, ordinary people show us how they handle adversity in an extraordinary way. We have only to think of the survivors of wars and concentration camps and the victims of floods, tornadoes, fires, hurricanes, and other disasters to realize the tremendous courage most people possess. During these times of tragedy, they somehow draw additional strength from their faith, families, and friends to help them meet and overcome obstacles. They refuse to become mired down in their troubles. Instead, like the confident little first grade reader, they just 'weed awound them' and keep on going.

Tee Carr

Jelly-Side Down

Blessed with four active children under five years old, I did everything I could to make them more independent. This was motivated in part because I wanted them to be self-reliant and in part from a more selfish desire to gain a few precious minutes for myself to wash my face or throw a load of clothes in the washer.

As small as my children were at the time, they were quick studies. They easily learned to pour milk over cereal, pick up toys and clothes, dress themselves, and make their own beds. However, I occasionally heard an *"Uh-oh, Mama"* coming from the kitchen at lunchtime when they were helping each other make sandwiches.

After hearing this one day, I entered the kitchen and saw four pairs of blue eyes staring intently at the floor. One of the three boys had dropped his slice of bread, and it had landed jelly-side down, creating a red, sticky, gooey mess. On seeing me, he said *"Uh-oh"* again and pointed to his accident.

Life teaches us many lessons, among them that even in the best of circumstances, a mishap can occur or the unforeseen can happen. We learn that some events cannot be anticipated or controlled.

All teachers have days that do not go as planned. They often tell me that fire drills, intercom announcements, an early snowfall, or a bird flying in the classroom window have disrupted some of their best lessons. Any of these incidents would cause a flurry of excitement among their students resulting in a loss of concentration on the finer points of reading, writing, or arithmetic.

The key to sanity lies in the way one reacts to these unanticipated events. Being able to adjust, switch gears, retain a sense of humor, and continue on are valuable skills. I don't know how "flexibility" is taught or even if it can be. Perhaps children learn this behavior by watching good parents and teachers model it. Perhaps they observe it in action by seeing grown-ups display a sense of humor and appear calm when serious situations go awry. No matter how we acquire these skills of adaptability, they are definitely ones that we should tuck into life's backpack to carry along with us when the road gets bumpy.

Sometimes the unforeseen event makes the situation more memorable. It marks the moment in our minds and gives us something to talk about or laugh about for years. If you want to guarantee rain, just schedule an outdoor wedding reception. I did, and *it did*. Just as our guests arrived, it began to sprinkle. We hurriedly moved the multi-tiered wedding cake, refreshments, and guests to the shelter of the big white canvas tent we had set up on the lawn. Then the band struck up their rendition of "Raindrops Keep Falling on My Head" and under colorful umbrellas, we danced right on.

Life will always have its sticky messes and unexpected happenings. Things will not always go as planned. We need to make sure we have on hand an ample reserve of strength, understanding, patience, and laughter to cope with those inevitable "jelly-side down" days.

Tee Carr

Part VIII

INSPIRATION

AND

ENCOURAGEMENT

Education is not filling a pail but the lighting of a fire.

William Butler Yeats
Irish Poet and Dramatist

Four Words That Changed a Life

"Are you too stupid to do anything right?" These words—said by a woman to a little boy who was evidently her son—were spoken because he had walked away from her. And they were said at a volume high enough that all the strangers in the vicinity could hear. Chastised, the boy returned quietly to the woman's side, his eyes downcast.

Not a big moment, perhaps. Yet small moments sometimes last a very long time. And a few words—though they mean little at the time to the people who say them—can have enormous power. "Are you too stupid to do anything right?" Words like that can echo.

I recently heard a story from a man named Malcolm Dalkoff. He's 48; for the last 24 years he has been a professional writer, mostly in advertising. Here is what he told me:

As a boy in Rock Island, Illinois, Dalkoff was terribly insecure and shy. He had few friends and no self-confidence. Then one day in October 1965, his high-school English teacher, Ruth Brauch, gave the class an assignment. The students had been reading *To Kill a Mockingbird.* Now they were to write their own chapter that would follow the last chapter of the novel.

Dalkoff wrote his chapter and turned it in. Today he cannot recall anything special about the chapter he wrote, or what grade Mrs. Brauch gave him. What he does remember—what he will never forget—are the four words Mrs. Brauch wrote in the margin of the paper: "This is good writing."

Four words. They changed his life.

"Until I read those words, I had no idea of who I was or what I was going to be," he said. "After reading her note, I went home and wrote a short story, something I had always dreamed of doing but never believed I could do."

Over the rest of that year in school, he wrote many short stories and always brought them to school for Mrs. Brauch to evaluate. She was encouraging, tough and honest. "She was just what I needed," Dalkoff said.

He was named co-editor of his high-school newspaper. His confidence grew; his horizons broadened; he started off on a successful, fulfilling life. Dalkoff is convinced that none of this would have happened had that woman not written those four words in the margin of his paper.

For his 30th high-school reunion, Dalkoff went back and visited Mrs. Brauch, who had retired. He told her what her four words had done for him. He told her that because she had given him the confidence to be a writer, he had been able to pass that confidence on to the woman who would become his wife, who became a writer herself. He told Mrs. Brauch that a young woman in his office, who was working in the evenings toward a high-school-equivalency diploma, had come to him for advice and assistance. She respected him because he was a writer—that is why she turned to him.

Mrs. Brauch was especially moved by the story of helping the young woman. "At that moment I think we both realized that Mrs. Brauch had cast an incredibly long shadow," he said.

"Are you too stupid to do anything right?"

"This is good writing."

So few words. They can change everything.

Bob Greene

A Remarkable Teacher

I was blessed in grade school with a beautiful young teacher who gave me divine inspiration throughout my whole life. Her name was Lois Cowan, and she was my teacher from the first through the sixth grade.

As a child of three I was placed, along with three of my brothers, in the Presbyterian Orphan's Home at Northside in Pittsburgh. The sudden death of my father left my mother with six children and very little money. Mother was a good seamstress, and she found a job in a clothing factory sewing trousers together. She placed her youngest children in the care of the orphanage since she often had to work twelve hours a day.

The Presbyterian Church of Pittsburgh ran the orphanage, and I was treated well. However, I missed my mother so much. I remember the first day I was taken to the Home. Although people say you don't have a memory of most things until you are about five, I definitely remember this incident. When my mother left me and my brothers, I ran to the large iron fence and tried to crawl through it to go home with her. I was crying all the while, and I suppose it broke her heart to see me in that condition as she turned to leave, walking through that huge gate.

My mother always visited us once a week on her day off even though she was busy at home taking care of her two older children. However, it was Lois Cowan who was my surrogate mother during those days of hardship for me. She looked after me constantly and her presence made up somewhat for the way I missed Mom.

When I became school age, the other children from the orphanage and I walked the eight blocks to school each day. I was sent to school neat and clean, but somehow, being a curious and active kid, I was constantly lured to other things along the way. I usually ended up arriving at school late with dirt all over my clothes, face, and hands. Miss Cowan always took me aside and cleaned me up. Throughout those early school years, she not only taught me to read and write, but she looked after me as if I were her own child.

When I finished high school, Miss Cowan attended my graduation. She counseled me when it was time to choose a college, and she was there to congratulate me upon receiving my degree. When the United States declared war on Japan and Germany in the early 40's, she actively encouraged me to enlist in the Army Air Corps to serve my country. A few years later, when I received my wings and was commissioned a lieutenant in the Air Corps, she was there for me.

In 1944, I was sent overseas to England where I flew 32 missions over Europe. All of this time, Miss Cowan kept in touch with me through her letters. I always recognized her beautiful, perfect handwriting on the envelopes and looked forward to her frequent and newsy letters.

Upon returning home from Europe, Miss Cowan was one of the first people I visited. I found her in a hospital recuperating from a stroke that left her paralyzed on her right side, severely affecting her ability to write. She never complained or let me know about this in her letters. She had learned to write with her left hand, and I never even suspected the difference.

Miss Lois Cowan never married but devoted her entire life to the teaching profession. She lived to be 95 and was one of the most remarkable women I have ever known. To this day, I miss her friendship and worthy counsel.

Ange Robbe

The Turning Point

From all accounts, Daddy didn't take to school much. His body was present in the classroom, but his mind was somewhere else. While his teachers talked of planets or foreign countries, he dreamed of fishing for bream off the river bank or riding the ebony pony on his cousin's farm.

He never gave his teachers any problems. Dreamers rarely do. He wasn't boisterous or disruptive. It was just that books and papers did not capture his attention. There were more interesting things on the other side of the schoolhouse door—frisky dogs chasing noisy June bugs, busy spiders spinning geometric webs, giant trees for climbing, and cool swimming holes.

Each year Daddy fell further and further behind his more industrious classmates. Most years he failed to be promoted to the next grade. Nevertheless, each bright and sunny September, he walked into the next grade's classroom and found himself a seat.

I don't know how he pulled this off. Perhaps the grade cards stating promotion or retention disappeared over the summer. Or perhaps the teachers were intimidated by the thought of having to confront his father with this problem since Granddaddy happened to be the county magistrate. For whatever reason, my daddy established his own policy of social promotion, and it seemed to work for him.

During his fourteenth summer, Daddy had a serious accident while riding a horse. It was galloping at a pretty fast pace when a wild rabbit frightened it, causing the horse to become skittish and suddenly change directions. The horse barreled into the barbed wire fence surrounding the property, causing the sharp barbs to rip savagely into my daddy's left leg.

For the next few weeks, the local doctor treated Daddy's wounds. However, the infection would not heal and gangrene seemed to be setting in. The doctor finally announced that there was a strong possibility that Daddy would lose his leg, and he would probably need to amputate it in a few days.

Around that same time, another doctor was traveling from Jacksonville to Washington to attend a medical convention. He stopped over in our town and spent the night at the local doctor's home. Back then there were no Holiday Inns. That night the two doctors swapped stories about some of their interesting cases, and they discussed my daddy's leg.

The next day the visiting doctor accompanied Daddy's doctor to see this "interesting case." The visiting doctor decided to extend his stay for a few days to treat Daddy with a new drug he had heard about.

Each day the doctor would visit Daddy, treat the wound, and then sit beside the bed having long conversations with his young patient. Daddy was full of questions—about medicine and diseases, about how the doctor decided what he wanted to do with his life, and what steps he took to accomplish this.

A week later, Daddy was up and about. His leg was healing nicely, so the visiting physician said goodbye and continued on his trip. Daddy's family commented about how healthy their son looked. They also noticed how he seemed to be more alert, more energized.

Daddy couldn't wait for school to start. He began to read and read—books, magazines, even the labels on the sides of pill bottles—anything and everything. When school resumed, he began to study with a vengeance. It was almost as if he were driven by a need to catch up on all that he had missed and by a desire to go forward.

When asked what he planned to do when high school was over, he stated confidently, "I'm going to go on to school and become a doctor."

And he did.

The young man who floundered so aimlessly during his early school years now had a goal—a mission—a passion for what he wanted to accomplish.

He had a plan to achieve that goal, and getting an education was a large part of that plan.   Sometimes lives are revitalized when given a direction.

In June of 1937, on an unbearably hot and humid summer day in Charleston, Walter Cecil Carnes donned his robes and graduated from the Medical College of the State of South Carolina.   On this day, my daddy realized his dream—he became a doctor.

Tee Carr

Dr. Bobby

During my freshman year at Chattanooga State Community College, I was determined that I was going to make straight "A's" on *every* test in *every* class. I know one of the reasons I was trying so hard to excel was because there were individuals who had told me I couldn't succeed.

Before I got my power wheelchair, I'd travel from class to class by "thumbing" rides from friends, other students, or fellow classmates. I'd hold out my thumb and students passing by would help by pushing my wheelchair! Between classes I always went to the Student Center to "catch up" on news with my friends and chat with Dr. Bobby. Dr. Bobby Smith was the Dean of Students at Chattanooga State, and he was always "checking in," as he called it, with the students.

One day I was sitting at the Student Center and Dr. Bobby asked, "What's wrong, Pam? You look like you've lost your best buddy." I told him I had failed my history test, and I was going to get a "C" in history. "They were right," I said. "I'm not cut out for college!"

We talked for a long time about the fact that I had studied and done my best, but I hadn't made the grade I wanted. I will never forget what he said to me: "Pam, nine out of ten employers hire "B" and "C" students. Employers know these students are well-rounded, will do their best, and are eager to learn more each day. Just keep giving it your best."

Dr. Bobby's words of encouragement remained with me all through my years in college. When it came time for me to graduate, Dr. Bobby, again, helped me with a potential problem. There were steps leading up to the stage where we were to receive our diplomas. I wanted to accept my degree on that stage just the same as my fellow students. Dr. Bobby came through for me. He requested permission from Dr. Charles Branch, President of Chattanooga State, to let the basketball team lift me in my power wheelchair onto the stage at graduation. After getting my sheepskin, each of my basketball "buddies" gave me a kiss and a rose. Oh, by the way, I had a 3.8 Grade Point Average and went on to graduate from Memphis State University.

Thanks to Dr. Bobby Smith always cheering me on, I now utilize that same spirit of encouragement in my work. I know that individuals who always do their best will be successful.

Pam Jackson

Red Sunsets

I cannot look at a red sunset without thinking about a first grade teacher in my school who was conducting an art lesson for her 26 wiggly charges. A student teacher from the local university was helping with the project. As principal, I was visiting this classroom and observing the teachers and children at work.

Most kindergarten and first grade budding artists color or paint the sky in their pictures at the top of the paper. It floats and hovers there like an airborne blue ribbon. On this day the teacher was trying to show her children that the sky included all of the area above the roofs and treetops. With her blue crayon and newsprint paper, she was demonstrating how to bring the sky down to meet the horizon line.

Kathy, the student teacher, mingled among the students, looking at their pictures and making positive comments. She noticed one little fellow standing at his table, working feverishly to color in his sky.

"Mrs. Adams," Kathy quietly said to the teacher, "Kenny is coloring his sky red. He must not have a blue crayon. I'll see if I can find one for him."

"No, Kathy, let's leave him alone for awhile," said the teacher, wise in the ways of children. "He seems to be so absorbed in his creation. And after all, it *is* his picture. It's possible that perhaps Kenny sees things differently from the other children."

Later in the day, I passed by the first grade classroom and observed the finished pictures hanging proudly in the hall. I had no trouble finding Kenny's. Twenty-five drawings had skies of various shades of blue, sporting fluffy white clouds of all sizes and shapes. The twenty-sixth picture was Kenny's red sunset. It sparkled like a jewel.

❦

Young children, by nature, are curious and creative. Anyone who has ever observed children at play knows that they can magically turn shoe boxes into chugging trains, hauling trucks, or speeding cars. In no time at all, kids can transform cardboard refrigerator cartons into playhouses or forts and play for hours and hours, immersed in their own special world.

All too often, however, as children grow older, their imaginations are stifled as adults tend to place more emphasis on turning out conformists rather than nurturing each individual's innate curiosity and creativity. And yet, all of the world's songs, poems, dances, plays, inventions, and services that enrich our lives originally sprang from the minds of creative people who were searching for new and better ways of doing or thinking about things.

We have all heard the story about young Ben Franklin who, even at play, was always exploring his world. When he and his playmates went swimming in the river, Ben would tie paddles on his feet so he could swim faster. Always thinking, always creating, Franklin grew up to become America's best-known innovator as well as a respected statesman, diplomat, printer, author, scientist, and inventor.

So what are the lessons that we as parents and teachers must learn? We must look closely at our homes and classrooms to see if we are providing an environment that encourages young people to think in new ways and try different approaches to problems without fear of disapproval or humiliation. By establishing a non-threatening learning climate, we will reassure our children that it is O.K. to diverge from the norm—to paint their skies a different color.

In addition, we must ensure that our young people have adequate time during the day to work on independent projects of their own choosing and have the freedom to proceed at their own pace. Children need time to think, to research, to create.

As adults, we must cease to believe that our way is the only way. We must listen to children and respect the decisions and choices they make as they grow and learn.

We must admire children's individuality and applaud their uniqueness. By encouraging creative and innovative thinking, we will expand the realm of possibilities for young people in their quest for learning.

We must, above all, celebrate and cherish red sunsets.

Tee Carr

Turning Boys into Men

Even before I reached Bill Eskridge's eighth grade English class at The McCallie School in Chattanooga, I already knew him fairly well.

His stated role was very straightforward: to give me a solid foundation in English grammar and literature. But he came to play a vastly greater role in my life than I could have possibly imagined then.

Growing up in East Ridge, Tennessee, and playing baseball, basketball, football and tennis, I had at least met Mr. Eskridge, who lived only a few blocks away from my home. Of course, nearly all of the neighborhood boys who liked sports as I did had heard of Bill Eskridge. If you had met him, even casually, you were not likely to forget the experience. He was colorful and direct. He had a reputation for toughness and discipline. He was somewhat of a loner, but his dedication to young people became a trademark as he molded boys into men.

As a teacher, he was firm but entertaining. He expected us to come to class well prepared, but in a sometimes eccentric manner, he kept our attention.

Like all great teachers, he taught us much more than the subject at hand. Partly by example, partly by inspiration, and very much by perspiration, Coach Eskridge taught me and countless other young men how to rise above our self-imposed limitations and through teamwork achieve greatness far above our own expectations.

He taught some of those lessons directly in the classroom. Each and every one of us memorized A. E. Housman's poem, "To an Athlete Dying Young." To reinforce its meaning, he had us recite the lines to our class. Nearly thirty years later, I still catch myself reciting those lines when I need encouragement and perspective.

There were rites of passage also. Each year, in the spring, Bill Eskridge took his eighth grade students to the persimmon tree on Missionary Ridge near McCallie. Eating a persimmon for the first time as a young man is an experience one definitely never forgets!

I learned the greatest lessons from Coach Eskridge, not in the classroom, but on the basketball court where he was McCallie's head coach from 1962 to 1983. He loved the game; and playing under him I developed a life-long passion, not just for the game of basketball, but for life itself. He taught me that if you set your goals high and are willing to dedicate yourself to excellence, you can accomplish much more than you could ever imagine.

Inspirationally, but not always gently, Bill Eskridge taught me how to reach down within myself to find strengths and abilities that I had no idea were there. He taught me that the great barrier to success is the fear of failure. Bill Eskridge taught me the meaning of the word "motivation"—literally—we all had to memorize it. Motivation: the stuff that permeates your entire being when you have a clear, vivid picture in your mind of what you want and an intense, burning, all-consuming desire in your heart to fight for it. Coach Eskridge taught me discipline, dedication, and mental toughness.

Perhaps most importantly, Bill Eskridge ingrained in me that no matter how well one does in life, one must maintain a sense of humility and purpose. He said that if we worked together unselfishly, we could beat teams with far more talent. So it is with life—the whole is greater that the sum of its parts.

Bill Eskridge was very good at what he did. But he was never overcome by the praise of others. After his retirement, he continued coaching basketball as a volunteer. Unfortunately, tragedy soon struck Coach Eskridge. One June morning in 1995, he was in his car just outside the gate of McCallie School on the way to continue his life's passion of teaching young boys the game of basketball—and so much else. But he never reached school that morning. In a random, senseless act, his car was struck by another car. His life ended before I could say goodbye to the teacher and coach who helped so much to make me the man I am today.

His life's work lives on through generations of boys whose path to manhood he shaped so powerfully. He trained us to accept nothing less than the best from ourselves. He encouraged us to thrive on challenges, to take joy in success and victory. But the most important lesson that he taught us is that if we work together, great things can happen.

Bill Eskridge never let us forget those lines from Housman learned long ago but never set aside:

> *And early though the laurel grows*
> *It withers quicker than the rose.*

Congressman Zack Wamp

A Sunny Place

"You may add anything that you want to our community mural as long as you make it better," I instructed each class before they added their paint, glitter, chalk, and collage. As I repeated these words to each art class, I thought—this would be good advice for our schools and for our world.

We began our mural by covering four walls from ceiling to floor with paper. My first classes were the city planners and engineers, designing the towns and planning the roads. We wanted farmland, lakes, neighborhoods, suburbs, and of course, a big city with towering skyscrapers.

One wall portrayed early morning in the country where a gigantic chalky sun rose over fields of sheep and tractors and lollipop trees. On another wall it was midday in towns and neighborhoods, and then there was nighttime in the big city. The classes that followed began filling the farmland with cows and horses, barns and apple trees. Houses and malls sprang up, and future architects designed innovative buildings with wallpaper, glue, and their endless imaginations.

We experienced changes throughout each day and throughout the project. Every morning students would detour on the way to their classes to see what new things had been added. They found mountain ranges and telephone poles, tree houses and helicopters, and even an erupting volcano. I heard that some of my last classes feared they would not get to add anything, so we changed seasons and the snows came. Winter brought snowflakes and glitter, snowmen and ice skaters, frozen ponds and snowball fights.

One fifth-grader smirked while asking, "Why are there so many suns in the sky?" Her fellow classmates giggled and others chimed in, "And when do you ever see an erupting volcano?" I thought back to the little

girl who came to me in tears and asked if she too could put her yellow paper sun in the sky, even though there was already one. Once I said yes to her, suns sprang up in the sky every day—chalky suns and painted suns, suns with pointed rays and wavy rays, suns of every color and shape. And then there were many moons, but everyone was happy and our mural began to take on a surreal, otherworldly look, a look I felt most comfortable with.

After all, we were a little community of artists creating a new community. It was a place bigger than ourselves, a place where ordinary scraps of paper build beautiful buildings, but also where monumental masterpieces stand beside crowded dull tenement houses with shutters that hang crooked and windows that are gray. It was a place where race cars travel beside pickup trucks and there are no one-way streets, a place where flowers grow bigger than people and roads go straight to the sky.

Where is this place where airplanes and kites, blackbirds and rockets, rainbows and snowflakes all exist in the same sky, and there's room for them all? As I walk through that hallway I am filled with joy and wonder and amazement. There's so much to see, so much to look at. I think—our schools can be like this.

School can be a place where children step out of an adult world of "shoulds" and "should nots" and enter into a world where their contributions are valued, even revered.   School can be a place where children feel assured that if they too want to make another sun, they may, because school is where people are receptive to changes and new ideas.   School can be a place where there are volcanoes beside swing sets and butterflies atop snowmen, where tree limbs embrace, and the sky holds many suns.

Beth Smithson

Contributors

Thanks again to the following individuals who shared their stories, poems, and anecdotes for this book.

Richard (Dick) Abrahamson, Ph.D., is Professor of Literature for Children and Young Adults at the University of Houston. Dr. Abrahamson is the winner of the Educational Press Association Award for Excellence in Educational Journalism. Each year he speaks to thousands of teachers on the topic of reading motivation and the reading interests of youngsters in grades K-12. Dr. Abrahamson can be reached at the University of Houston, Department of Curriculum and Instruction, Houston, Texas 77204-5872.

Curtis Adams enjoyed a fun-filled career of 41 years with the *Chattanooga News Free Press*. He is president of Adams Tire Center. He is also president of the East Ridge Chamber of Commerce. Curtis Adams is known as the Education Commissioner on the Hamilton County Commission. In his 12 years of service, Commissioner Adams has visited each of Hamilton County's 81 schools and has been a speaker for 235 different groups. One of his proudest achievements is the Pioneer Frontier Playground in East Ridge which displays a plaque in his honor at the location. He runs advertisements each year in the newspaper saluting his heroes—school teachers. He and his wife, Dot, have four children and eight grandchildren.

Lee Anderson is associate publisher and editor of the *Chattanooga Free Press and Chattanooga Times*. He joined the newspaper at the age of 16 while a junior in high school. He has won 26 Freedoms Foundation awards including the 1979 prize for the top editorial in the nation. Among his other numerous awards are the Kiwanis Distinguished Service Award for 1995, the Chattanooga Bar Association's Liberty Bell Award, and in 1987, Lee was presented the first national James Monroe Foundation Editorial Award in Washington, D.C. He is a retired major in the Army Reserve. Lee Anderson is married, has two daughters and two grandchildren and lives on Missionary Ridge.

Elizabeth Silance Ballard is a freelance writer whose short stories and articles have been published in many periodicals and book anthologies since 1975. She enjoys reading and travel, especially foreign travel, and being with her grandchildren, Joshua and Tiffany. She works with the Virginia Department of Social Services and lives with her husband, Sam, in Virginia Beach.

Erma Bombeck (1927-1996) was one of America's favorite and best-loved humorists. Millions felt that they "knew" her as the Mom next door or a favorite aunt, but had only met her through her columns or books. She published more than four thousand syndicated articles in her column "At Wit's End" from 1965 until her death on April 22, 1996. Erma Bombeck was a regular on ABC-TV's "Good Morning America." She wrote over a dozen books, her best known entitled *The Grass is Always Greener Over the Septic Tank* that was later made into a movie.

Fran Buttolph, now retired, was a teacher for seven years and a principal for 21 years in the Fulton County School System in Atlanta, Georgia. During her last 14 years as the principal at Esther Jackson Elementary School in Roswell, Georgia, the school was twice recognized as a Georgia School of Excellence. She and her husband live in Atlanta. They enjoy bridge, square dancing, and traveling.

Paula M. Carnes taught sixth grade, reading, and Bible for 18 years. After developing Chronic Fatigue Syndome, she began tutoring homebound students. Paula is an inspirational speaker on living life to the fullest in spite of chronic illness. Contact her at PaulaJeanne@InfoAve.net.

Pete Carnes is a retired educator, having served thirty years as a teacher in the public schools in Tennessee and South Carolina. He taught in grades five through high school level including two years as a guidance counselor. He is presently the Chief of State Constables (a volunteer police agency) for Lancaster County and holds the rank of Lieutenant. For the past two years, he has worked for the Department of Corrections. He was a Scout Master and the proud father of two successful sons.

David Carroll is news anchor and "School Patrol" reporter for WRCB-TV, the NBC affiliate in Chattanooga, Tennessee. He and his wife Cindy have two sons, Chris and Vince. He is the recipient of the Tennessee Education Association School Bell Award and three "Excellence In Education Reporting" awards from the Tennessee School Boards Association.

Wes Castle is a third year teacher in the Hamilton County School System in Chattanooga, Tennessee. He is currently teaching first grade at Barger Academy of Fine Arts. He and his wife Amy enjoy outdoor activities such as hiking, running, and camping.

Pat Conroy is one of America's favorite storytellers. His rare gifts of language, passion, and abundant good humor are well known to his followers. Among his works are *The Water Is Wide, The Great Santini, The Lords of Discipline, Beach Music,* and *The Prince of Tides.* Much of his work is autobiographical and since Conroy was raised in the South, he incorporates much of the southern culture in his novels. *The Water Is Wide* gives an account of his early teaching days in a poor school located on an island off the coast of South Carolina. The movie version was called *Conrack* and starred Jon Voight.

Bill (William Henry, Jr.) Cosby, Ed.D., is a comedian, author, actor, and television producer. A teacher at heart, he received his doctorate in education at age 39 in 1977. Dr. Cosby's interest in children and education led him to incorporate many of his ideas and ideals in his work. His production of *Fat Albert and the Cosby Kids* entertained and instructed countless children of all ages. This father of five has delighted generations with his special brand of humor and wisdom. Currently he stars in the sitcom *Cosby* and hosts the show *Kids Say the Darndest Things.* His gentle, wry clowning, which appeals to both children and adults, led to a series of successful television commercials, comedy records, and books, and made him one of the wealthiest individuals in the history of the American entertainment industry.

Jewell Baldwin Cousin enjoyed 39 years as a teacher, supervisor, director, and principal in the Chattanooga Public Schools. Her interest in teaching students of varying ages led her to work at the elementary, junior high, and high school levels, as well as at the Occupational Training Center which was for students who were 18-25 years of age. Since her retirement, Mrs. Cousin has been involved in volunteer work and has become an avid bridge player.

Herb Criswell sold his business and retired in 1991. He describes himself as an enthusiastic, if untalented, golfer. He is married to Carolyn, a retired school teacher. They have three successful children and three grandchildren. They enjoy retirement in Signal Mountain, Tennessee. To comment on Herb's story, you can e-mail him at *Hcris51553@aol.com.*

Terrence E. (Terry) Deal, Ph.D., is the author and co-author of twenty books (*The New Corporate Cultures, Leading With Soul, Shaping School Culture,* to name a few) and more than 100 articles and book chapters concerning organizations, leadership, change, culture, symbolism, and spirit. A former teacher, principal, cop, and administrator, he specializes in the study of organizations and offers consulting services to a wide variety of organizations in the United States and abroad. Dr. Deal is the recipient of numerous awards and honors such as Vanderbilt's Distinguished Professor Award (1996), The University of La Verne Alumnus of the Year (1997), and the ASCD Affiliate Excellence Award (1996) for an Outstanding Contribution to Education.

Jackie Elkins retired from the Chattanooga School System in 1985 with 30 years of service in various positions. She received the ACE Elementary Teacher Award and the American Cancer Tennessee National Life Saver Award. She has served on the boards of the Houston Museum, Northside Neighborhood House, American Cancer Society, and is a member of Delta Kappa Gamma and First Baptist Church. Jackie and her husband, Joe, are natives of Chattanooga and the parents of two children.

Meagan Nichole Floyd is a student at Battlefield Elementary School in Catoosa County, Georgia. She is interested in basketball, reading, shopping, and swimming. She is a pitcher for a local girls' fast pitch softball team. When she grows up, Meagan plans to become a lawyer.

Frances Forester is a hairdresser who has lived and worked in the Chattanooga Valley vicinity for over 50 years. She married her husband, Lake, who was in the service, before he went to Germany. She and Lake (now deceased) have two daughters, Nancy and Margarete Ann. Frances enjoys her four grandchildren and two great-grandchildren. She also enjoys dancing, sewing, and gardening. She presently resides in Rossville, Georgia.

Robert Fulghum is a natural-born storyteller. As a philosopher and essayist, he shares uncommon thoughts on common things in his bestselling books, *All I Really Need to Know I Learned in Kindergarten, It Was on Fire When I Lay Down on It, Uh-Oh,* and *Maybe (Maybe Not).* Robert Fulghum has been a working cowboy, IBM salesman, professional artist, folksinger, parish minister, bartender, and teacher of drawing and painting. He divides his time between Seattle and Utah.

Ann Marie Furr is a middle school student at Mt. Pleasant, North Carolina. She enjoys tumbling, riding horses, dancing, and cheering. She will be completing her ninth year of dance this year. Ann Marie wants to attend Duke University and become a registered nurse.

Haim Ginott, Ed.D., (1922-1973) was a clinical psychologist, child therapist, and parent educator whose bestselling books, *Between Parent and Child* (1955), *Group Psychotherapy with Children* (1961), *Between Parent and Teenager* (1969), and *Teacher and Child* (1972), revolutionized the way child therapists, parents, and teachers relate to children. The communication skills that Dr. Ginott advocated help teachers, parents, and others who work with young people become more capable of compassion, caring, and commitment.

Sammy Gooden retired from the Chattanooga Public School System after 39 years as a teacher, principal, and area director of schools. He is married and has two daughters. He served on the Tennessee State Committee for the Southern Association of Colleges and Schools and continues to work as a SACS consultant.

Bob Greene is a syndicated newspaper columnist, broadcast television correspondent, author, and child advocate. He was the recipient of the National Headline Award for best newspaper column in the United States in 1977 and the Peter Lisagor Award for 1981. Among his books are *American Beat*, 1983; *Cheeseburger: The Best of Bob Greene*, 1985; *Be True to Your School*, 1987; and his latest, *Duty*, 2000.

Jack Greenstein was an elementary school teacher and principal for 23 years. After he retired he wrote *What the Children Taught Me*, an anecdotal account of his experiences as an educator. A Japanese translation was published in Tokyo in 1989. For the past nine years Jack has been giving talks to elementary school students on topics such as smoking, alcohol, illegal drugs, peer pressure, and race relations.

Lewis Grizzard (1946-1994), a great American, who described himself as a "quintessential southern male," was a writer, lecturer, entertainer, and a syndicated columnist for the *Atlanta Journal* and *Constitution*. He wrote more than a dozen books including *Kathy Sue Loudermilk, I Love You* and *Won't You Come Home, Billy Bob Bailey?* Through his writings, he gave us his special mixture of humor, sentiment, satire, and down-home philosophizing while immortalizing his hometown of Moreland, Georgia, and its inhabitants. Grizzard was among the most successful and insightful contemporary observers of the changing South.

Brent Hall is the senior minister at Brainerd United Methodist Church in Chattanooga, Tennessee. He has served as Growth Plus Consultant for many churches in the Holston Conference. Brent and his wife, Vicki, have three grown children. Throughout his ministry, he has helped develop and improve Learning Center ministries for children.

John Hartford is a musician, songwriter, and entertainer. He won two Grammy Awards in 1967 for his "Gentle on My Mind" which was to be recorded and broadcast more than any other song. Hartford has recorded over 30 albums including the 1976 Grammy winner, *Mark Twang.* Hartford is a powerful voice for his twin muses, the river and its music. He is known for his one-man shows performed on riverboats. In 1999, he was inducted into the St. Louis Hall of Fame.

Shane Harwood is a 24-year-old, first year physical education teacher in the Hamilton County School System. He also coaches high school basketball and is currently pursuing a master's degree in School Administration. Shane enjoys travel and writing. He is also planning to publish a book and calendar providing insight for other beginning teachers entering the field of education.

Eunice C. Hodges serves as principal of DuPont Elementary School with the Hamilton County School system in Chattanooga, Tennessee. A twenty-year veteran in public education, she has been an early childhood educator and has presented reading and mathematics workshops on the local and state levels. The DuPont PTA presented her the PTA Lifetime Membership Award in February 2000. Eunice has two children, three grandchildren, and resides on Signal Mountain.

Vickie Honeycutt has taught English at Mt. Pleasant High School for 31 years. In 1987, she designed and implemented the curriculum for one of North Carolina's first high school Teacher Cadet programs. She was also instrumental in the initiation of the Cabarrus County Freshman Seminar program for which she now serves as the lead teacher. She was recently named Southwest Regional Teacher of the Year and is one of six finalists for North Carolina State Teacher of the Year. She is married and has two children, Ashley and Dane. She and her husband, Alan, reside in Mt. Pleasant, North Carolina.

Deborah Horton has successfully taught kindergarten for 12 years in the Chattanooga City and Hamilton County School Systems. She is married and has one son. She and her husband, Stephen, and son, Sam, live in Chattanooga, Tennessee. She enjoys reading, exercising, church, and spending time with her family.

Pam Jackson is the Independent Living Supervisor for Tri-State Resource and Advocacy Corporation, Inc., (TRAC) in Chattanooga, Tennessee. TRAC is a non-profit organization which assists individuals with disabilities through information and referrals, peer support, community and systems advocacy, and training for independent living skills. Pam enjoys people, outdoor activities, writing, and listening to music. She has received numerous awards for her contributions throughout the state of Tennessee. She can be contacted for presentations at *pj570@juno.com* or (423) 892-4774 (w) or (423) 698-6079.

Linda Green Johnson is a veteran educator of 25 years. Although her career has included pre-school, special education, and school psychology, she readily admits that the first grade classroom is her love. She and her husband, Donald, a middle school principal, live in Dunlap, Tennessee, with their two teenage children.

Connie Jones (alias Ms. Connie) began teaching in 1968. She has a B. S. degree in Art Education and a Master's degree in Diagnostic Prescriptive Teaching. She has taught at almost all levels. Her present position is with the Hamilton County Schools in a CDC-MH (Comprehensive Developmental Class—Multi Handicapped) classroom. She is known for her "C"reativity and her "C"razy alter ego, Ms. Wizard, a character she created who helps to make learning fun!

Martha Dyer Kaiser has received many honors in her 28 years in the teaching field. She was named the Hamilton County Education Association Teacher of the Year in 1987, the Elementary Teacher Making a Difference in 1990, the Hamilton County Teacher of the Year in 1995, and competed for the State Teacher of the Year in 1995. Martha is the former president of the Freedoms Foundation, and she is presently serving as the state chairperson for the Teachers Study Council in Tennessee. She has three sons. She and her husband, John, reside in Chattanooga. They enjoy their grandchildren, entertaining friends, dancing, playing golf, and traveling.

Linda Knowles, an educator for 33 years, is Staff Development Coordinator for Hamilton County Schools. She has been a member of many educational organizations including ASCD, National Staff Development Council, International Reading Association, and she has served as state president of the Tennessee Reading Association. Linda is the mother of four wonderful young adults and the grandmother of two beautiful children.

Darwin Lane is a retiree from the Chattanooga Public Schools. His career spanned 40 years, 37 as an elementary school principal. He is married and has four sons, the eldest one now teaching and coaching two sports. He and his wife, Joyce, reside in Chattanooga where he is active in the local retired teachers association.

L. Quentin Lane, Ed.D., is a retired educator and President Emeritus of Cleveland State Community College in Cleveland, Tennessee. He served as a teacher, counselor, assistant principal, principal, and director of staff personnel services in the Chattanooga Public Schools. Dr. Lane was director of public relations for the Tennessee Education Association. In addition, he served as dean of academic affairs, vice president for university relations and development, executive vice president, and president in five different institutions of higher education in Tennessee, Florida, and South Carolina. Dr. Lane is currently serving with the United Census Bureau as the Assistant Manager for Field Operations in twenty Tennessee counties. He and his wife, Evelyn, currently reside in Fairfield Glade, Tennessee.

Dorothy R. Leader received many awards during her 38 years with the Hamilton County School System in Tennessee. She is most proud of the two PTA Life Memberships presented to her, the Excellence in Education awards from two former Tennessee governors, and a joint resolution by the Tennessee

House and Senate commending her accomplishments and honoring her retirement. The high school seniors selected her as one of their most influential teachers. Since retiring, she has been honored by the Hamilton County Department of Education for her volunteer help with the Character Education Program.

Luaine Lee was born in Nebraska and moved to California with her parents when she was six. Her journalistic career began as a freelance photographer in Africa where she spent four years. After her return to the United States, she worked as a general assignment reporter and photographer and then became entertainment editor for a Los Angeles metropolitan daily. During her 17-year term as editor she covered all facets of show business: theater, television, movies, books, and travel. She began conducting celebrity interviews in the late '80s and has continuted to interpret Hollywood through the luminaries who populate it.

Angie Martin is a fifth grade teacher in Concord, North Carolina, who has enjoyed the teaching profession for nine years in Cabarrus County. She loves to write and has entered the North Carolina Young Authors Contest with her students each year. She has won at county and state levels. She currently resides in Harrisburg with her husband and daughter—a budding young author.

Laurie Massey McCall can't believe that she gets paid for teaching! After all, this is exactly what she did without pay while staying home with her own four children under the age of five. She was graciously accepted into the world of elementary public education at the seasoned age of 33 when her children were safely ensconced in pre-school, kindergarten, and first grade. Laurie has successful teaching experience in inner-city schools as well as the suburbs. Now, with her children carefully tucked away in various and sundry ivy-covered halls, Laurie is completing an Ed.S. degree and looking forward to tackling a master's in English.

Catherine Berry Sharp Memory taught elementary school in Dekalb County, Georgia, and Duval County, Florida. She now resides in Blackshear, Georgia. She has four children and nine grandchildren. Mrs. Memory says that since she is in her eighties, she gets a little tired sometimes, but she is not "retired" because she is still active, teaches Sunday School, and cherishes the members of her family—her *real* "Memorys."

Elspeth Campbell Murphy is the author of the well-known and bestselling books, *Recess* and *Chalkboard, Prayer Meditations for Teachers.* She was a first grade teacher in the low country of South Carolina. She now lives in Chicago and writes children's books. *Recess* and *Chalkboard* have been a source of inspiration to countless teachers.

Elizabeth Musico is an elementary student in Wallkill, New York. Her favorite subject is English, especially writing stories. She enjoys dancing and shopping, and watching basketball and baseball. When she grows up, she wants to be a teacher and a mother.

Katie Myers is a student at Soddy Daisy Middle School in Soddy, Tennessee. She enjoys playing the piano and the flute. She also enjoys reading, shopping, and most sports, including track. Katie is a straight "A" student and plans to attend college when she is older.

Stephen Myers is a student at Western Hills Elementary School in Denver, Colorado. He enjoys boating, soccer, track, and building model cars and trucks. He also enjoys school, especially typing on the computer in the lab. He is thinking about a career in the Navy.

Mike O'Brien is pastor of Mt. Pleasant United Methodist Church in North Carolina. Prior to this, he was chief of student affairs at colleges in Tennessee, North Carolina, and Pennsylvania for twenty years. Mike makes pottery, walking sticks, and is a storyteller in schools, colleges, and libraries. He is married and has three grown children.

Janet Ginsberg Perfetti taught elementary gifted students in the Chattanooga Public Schools from 1983-1988. She was active in CEA, served as Chattanooga space week coordinator, published articles, and won several honors along with her students. She may best be remembered for the 35-foot replica of the Statue of Liberty at Barger Elementary School that her students built to commemorate a fundraising project during the restoration. She is the widow of a most special teacher and principal, Louis B. Perfetti. Ms. Perfetti currently distributes themed party and novelty items and can be contacted at *PartyOrder@aol.com* or (423) 894-5567.

Lauren Rickey, Ed.D., lives in Tennessee with her husband, Michael, who is also in education. Lauren currently serves as an administrator in her local school system at a Special Day School for children with significant learning disabilities in grades K-12. Holding to the belief that there is a reason for all behavior, Dr. Rickey specializes in addressing children's behavioral challenges. She can be contacted for consultation and workshops at *Lrickey@aol.com* or by writing her at 1040 Tulip Grove Road, Hermitage, Tennessee. Currently, she is writing a work of encouragement for teachers with publication expected within the year 2000.

Barbara Rigsby has been an educator for 24 years as a classroom teacher and a Title I teacher. She is currently the assistant principal at Griffith Elementary School in Sequatchie County. She and her husband, Jim, have two sons, two daughters-in-law, and one precious grandson. They all reside in Soddy Daisy, Tennessee.

Ange Robbe was the Supervising Special Agent for the Federal Bureau of Investigation for 30 years. He is married and has two daughters. Ange is now retired and lives in Atlanta, Georgia, with his wife, Charlotte. His interests are music, tennis, photography, and travel.

Dalton Roberts is a teacher, humorist, musician, songwriter, newspaper columnist, and front porch philosopher. In 16 years as County Executive, his administration won over 100 national awards. He was chosen by the National Management Association as Manager of the Year in 1991. The University of Tennessee at Chattanooga established a professorship in public administration in his name. He performs over 100 times a year as "the downhome funosopher from downtown Watering Trough, Tennessee," and can be reached at *DownhomeP@aol.com* or 423-697-0680.

Gladys Robinson, Ed.D., retired in 1985 after serving the Lancaster County School System in Lancaster, South Carolina, for 46 years as a teacher, guidance counselor, and administrator. Prior to her retirement, Dr. Robinson was president of the Department of Classroom Teachers and the South Carolina representative for the Board of Directors of the Education Association. Dr. Robinson said, "My mom, some of my aunts, and an uncle were all teachers. I just grew up in a family where we were teachers. I didn't know there was any other profession."

Jeff Scott is a fifth grade teacher at Ringgold Elementary School. He received a master's degree in school administration from the University of Tennessee at Chattanooga. Some of Jeff's favorite interests are reading, exercising, and following politics. Jeff currently resides in Chattanooga, Tennessee.

Caitlin Schroeder is a student at the Chattanooga School for Liberal Arts in Tennessee. She plays the flute and dances on pointe. She is also an active member in the Children's International Summer Villages. Caitlin states that this is the first story of hers that has ever been published in a book.

Shel Silverstein (1932-1999) was a cartoonist, composer, lyricist, folksinger, and writer. He was best known for his collections of children's poetry, *Where the Sidewalk Ends: The Poems and Drawings of Shel Silverstein* and *A Light in the Attic*, both of which enjoyed extended stays on the *New York Times* bestseller list. He is also the author of *The Giving Tree* and numerous other books. In addition to his writings for children, Silverstein served as a longtime *Playboy* cartoonist, wrote several plays for adults, and penned and recorded such country and novelty songs as Johnny Cash's "A Boy Named Sue." Since his work transcended age and gender, it probably touched the lives of more people than any other writer in the second half of the 20th Century.

Natalie Smith is a student from Mt. Pleasant, North Carolina. She has a younger sister named Ashley, a dog named Annie, and two cats. She enjoys arts, crafts, soccer, and swimming. Natalie was chosen to attend S.P.E.C. camp in the summer of '99 and traveled to Washington, DC, in April 2000, with the school Student Council. Someday she plans to become a dentist.

Beth Smithson has been teaching art to the children of Mt. Pleasant Elementary School in North Carolina for 13 years. She lives in Concord, North Carolina, with her husband, Terry. They have two daughters—Tara, who attends the University of North Carolina at Chapel Hill, and Holly, who attends the College of Charleston in South Carolina. Beth is proud to be the daughter of Tee Carr, author of this book.

Jean Mizer Todhunter (1919-1998), author of "Cipher in the Snow," was a writer, world traveler and—most of all—a teacher. She had no children of her own so her students received her full attention. She was a talented, creative teacher who strived to instill each student with her love of education. Mrs. Todhunter lived her entire life in Hailey, Idaho, in a home built by her grandfather. She died at home on April 3, 1998.

Ann Tolstoy enjoyed 45 consecutive years as an educator, both as an English teacher and staff development instructor and consultant. She and her husband live in California. They have one daughter and one grandson. Ann is now retired and loves to travel. In her spare time she enjoys hiking, biking, water sports, and reading.

Sharon Richards Vaughn is a system curriculum facilitator for the Hamilton County schools. She is in her 29th year of teaching and is currently attending graduate school to earn an additional master's degree. She lives in Chattanooga with her husband, Ron, and two teenage children, Abby and Aaron.

Congressman Zack Wamp was elected to Congress in 1995 after a successful career as a commercial realty broker in Chattanooga. He was elected by the Republican Freshman

Class of 1994 as its representative on the Majority Steering Committee. Congressman Wamp was the first Tennessee Republican to be named to the House Appropriations Committee since 1910. He graduated from McCallie School in Chattanooga and attended the University of North Carolina at Chapel Hill and the University of Tennessee. He and his wife, Kim, have a son, Weston, and a daughter, Coty. They belong to Red Bank Baptist Church.

Anne Knight Watson teaches second grade at W. M. Irvin Elementary School in Concord, North Carolina. She has had a varied career, always reserving time to be with her family. She taught Chapter I reading classes for which she was recognized as the county's Reading Teacher of the Year. In addition, she taught Children's Literature at a nearby college and worked on a book for the cancer patients of a local medical clinic. Anne says that the hurly-burly of the regular classroom draws her now to the most spirited and rewarding teaching of her career.

George Whedbee spent 31 years in the Knoxville and Knox County School System. He served as a teacher, assistant principal, director of area vocational technical schools, business manager, and assistant superintendent for business affairs. George is married and has two daughters and two grandsons. He retired from the public schools in 1993. He is currently a marketing representative for Kaatz, Binkley, Jones, and Morris, Architects.

Cheryl Whiteley is the mother of two girls, Chara and Meara, who seem to be growing up much too fast. Chara is presently in kindergarten and Meara will be entering soon. Cheryl's understanding husband, Ken, is learning to adapt to her pre-empty nest syndrome. Cheryl, Ken, and their girls reside in Hixson, Tennessee. Cheryl is employed by R. Wiley Carr, DDS.

Oprah Winfrey is one of America's most beloved entertainers as well as the richest and most powerful person on television. *The Oprah Winfrey Show* is watched today by 33 million viewers. In 1996, she started her book club, creating instant bestsellers. Her role in *The Color Purple* launched her career as a movie actor and producer. In addition to these many endeavors, she is a humanitarian and a spokesperson for legislation for the protection of children.

Harry K. Wong, Ed.D., is one of the most sought after speakers in education today. Dr. Wong has been called Mr. Practicality for his common-sense, user-friendly, no-cost approach to managing a classroom for high-level student success. Together with his wife, Rosemary, they have written a book, *The First Days of School*, which has sold over one million copies.

Permissions

I would like to acknowledge the following publishers and individuals for granting permission to reprint the following material. Stories that were penned anonymously, that are public domain, or were written by me, are not included in this listing.

(continued from page ii)

The Letter. Reprinted by permission of W. C. (Pete) Carnes. ©2000 W. C. (Pete) Carnes.

What It Means to Teach. Reprinted by permission of Jeff L. Scott. ©2000 Jeff L. Scott.

I Have Come to a Frightening Conclusion excerpt by Haim Ginott from *TEACHER AND CHILD,* New York: Collier Books, 1993. Reprinted by permission of Alice Ginott. ©1973 Haim Ginott.

In Praise of a Teacher from *RECESS* by Elspeth Campbell Murphy. Reprinted by permission of Baker Book House, Grand Rapids, Michigan, 1992. ©1988 Elspeth Campbell Murphy.

The Seed. Reprinted by permission of Angie Martin. ©2000 Angie Martin.

Excerpt from *DON'T FORGET TO CALL YOUR MAMA . . . I WISH I COULD CALL MINE* by Lewis Grizzard, Longstreet Press, Inc., 1994. Reprinted by permission of the Estate of Lewis Grizzard. ©1991 Lewis Grizzard.

I Love You, Miss Patten. Reprinted by permission of Lee Anderson. ©2000 Lee Anderson.

Oprah on Teaching. Excerpts by Oprah Winfrey in *THE UNCOMMON WISDOM OF OPRAH WINFREY: A PORTRAIT IN HER OWN WORDS,* edited by Bill Adler. Reprinted by permission of Carol Publishing Group, Secaucus, NJ, 1997. ©Bill Adler 1997.

Miss Ferris by John Hartford from the album *HEADIN' DOWN INTO THE MYSTERY BELOW.* Reprinted by permission of John Hartford, John Hartford Music, Madison, TN. ©John Hartford.

She Makes Learning Fun. Reprinted by permission of Elizabeth Grace Musico. ©2000 Elizabeth Grace Musico.

Book Order Form

If you have enjoyed *School Bells and Inkwells*, you will want to purchase Tee's other books about teachers and children, *All Eyes Up Here! A Portrait of Effective Teaching* and *How Come The Wise Men Are In The DEMPSTER DUMPSTER®?* Please complete the order form below and send it with your check or money order to CARR Enterprises.

I'd like _____ copies of *School Bells and Inkwells* @ $14.95

I'd like _____ copies of *All Eyes Up Here!* @ $14.95

I'd like _____ copies of *How Come the Wise Men Are In The DEMPSTER DUMPSTER®?* @ $10.95

Shipping & Handling $2 for first book, $1.50 for additional copies.

My check or money order payable to CARR Enterprises for $_____ is enclosed.

Please print:

Name: _____

Address: _____

City/State/Zip: _____

Telephone Area Code/Number: _____

Purchase Orders welcome.

Quantity Discounts Available

For educational or quantity discounts, call 423-698-5685 or FAX 423-698-3182.

CARR Enterprises
3 Belvoir Circle
Chattanooga, TN 37412

E-Mail: drtcarr@aol.com